GM's GEEPS
The General Purpose Diesels

PAUL D. SCHNEIDER

KALMBACH
BOOKS

Dedication

For my old friend Ronald A. Plazzotta, railfan and locomotive roster shooter, who admonished me for years to "shoot dem Geeps!" when I had a tendency to take GP7s, 9s, and 18s for granted. Thanks, Ronnie!

© 2001 Kalmbach Publishing Co. All rights reserved. This book may not be reproduced in part or in whole without written permission of the publisher, except in the case of brief quotations used in reviews. Published by Kalmbach Publishing Co., 21027 Crossroads Circle, Waukesha, WI 53187.

Printed in the United States of America

01 02 03 04 05 06 07 08 09   10 9 8 7 6 5 4 3 2 1

Visit our website at
http://kalmbachbooks.com
Secure online ordering available

Publisher's Cataloging-in-Publication
(Provided by Quality Books, Inc.)

Schneider, Paul D.
    GM's Geeps : the general purpose diesels / Paul D. Schneider. — 1st ed.
      p. cm. — (Classic trains: the golden years of railroading)
    Includes index.

    1. Diesel locomotives—United States. 2. Diesel locomotives—Canada. 3. General Motors Corporation. I. Title.

TJ619.2.S36 2001   625.2'63'097
                              QBI01-700217

Art director: Kristi Ludwig
Book design: Sabine Beaupré

On the cover: EMD GP7 No. 100, the world's very first Geep. Electro-Motive photo

Contents

Geep Genesis 4

Hit the Road, Jack: Geep Demonstrators 9

EMD Geeps, Model by Model 12

   Have It Your Way: Geep Factory Options 19

Geeps Hard at Work 20

Geeps Today 124

Acknowledgments 126

Index of Photographs 127

Geep Genesis

▶ Described by *Trains* magazine editor David P. Morgan as "a cross between a cab unit and a Borden milk car," EMD's BL2 set the stage, albeit awkwardly, for the GP7's debut. Chesapeake & Ohio 83 is one of 59 BL2s built between February 1948 and May 1949. Louis A. Marre photo

Locomotive builder Electro-Motive's FT diesel is rightly known as "the diesel that did it." When the 5,400-horsepower four-unit locomotive rolled out of the builder's McCook, Illinois, plant in November 1939, it drove the first nail in the steam locomotive's coffin.

General Motors purchased Electro-Motive Corporation in 1930, and the locomotive builder came to be known as the Electro-Motive Division of General Motors, or EMD. Although other locomotive builders ultimately joined the fray, EMD's streamlined F units were largely responsible for bumping steam engines off the nation's mainline freight trains.

Successful as it was, the F unit proved less than ideal for local freight work. Here, the F's limited rear visibility and lack of steps and footboards made it a poor choice for switching. As steam retrenched to branch lines and locals and other builders moved to fill the need for non-road-freight diesels, EMD drew up plans for a new product, the "Branch Line."

With the "BL1," EMD stuffed the mechanical innards of a 1,500-horsepower F3 into a semistreamlined carbody that allowed better rear visibility. Switching was improved by the addition of footboards and end platforms. An optional steam generator allowed the unit to be used in local passenger service. At other times, it doubled as a local freight engine. After a lone "BL1" prototype, the model was changed to BL2.

Mind you, the road-switcher concept was hardly new when EMD launched the Branch Line in 1948. Legend has it the president of the Chicago, Rock Island & Pacific Railway sketched out the road-switcher concept on the back of an envelope in the early 1940s. Electro-Motive rival American Locomotive Company (often shortened to just "Alco") responded with a 1,000-horsepower dual-service locomotive eventually dubbed the RS-1.

Alco's formula was simple: Take one 1,000-horsepower S-2 switcher,

lengthen the underframe, add a short hood behind the cab (to house a steam generator for passenger service) and swap the hard-riding AAR Type A switcher trucks with Type B road trucks. Built between 1941 and 1960, the RS-1 lived up to its promise, proving equally at home in switching, road freight, local passenger, and commuter train service.

As it turned out, the BL2 was a stutter-step for EMD. In concept and execution it was a compromise that pleased neither railroaders nor EMD Service Department representatives. Perhaps the biggest problem was the semi-streamlined carbody, which was costly to produce and hampered routine service and repair work. It wasn't until 1949 that EMD came up with the right answer to the question of a general-purpose locomotive, the GP7.

The GP7 debuts

The GP7 wonderfully illustrates the design philosophy "Form follows function." EMD Chief Engineer Dick Dilworth came up with a functional design bereft of what he called "Christmas tree ornaments and other whimsy." The GP7 combined the proven machinery of a 1,500-horsepower F7 cab unit with the maintenance advantages of a hood-type superstructure. A short hood provided space for a steam generator for passenger service. This configuration allowed easy access for repair and service as well as improved visibility for crewmembers.

The GP7 took its name from "General Purpose" and soon acquired the nickname "Geep," much to the chagrin of EMD's General Manager at the time. To him, a Geep was a four-wheel-drive military vehicle (that is, a Jeep); as a result, he banned use of the name "Geep" within the company. Like reverse psychology, the ban only ensured continued use of the word "Geep" outside of the General Manager's office.

Today "Geep" customarily signifies models GP7, GP9, and GP18, which all share similar 567 engines and virtually identical carbody configuration. While later four-motor EMDs carry the GP designation and are often called "Geeps," the three early models are the focus of our study.

◀ Gulf, Mobile & Ohio RS-1 1116 stands at Peoria, Illinois, in April 1948. Generally regarded as the first true "road-switcher" diesel, Alco's RS-1 debuted in 1941, six years before EMD rolled out the first GP7. Although GM&O owned EMD cab units, the railroad never owned a Geep. Paul Stringham photo

Hit the Road, Jack: Geep Demonstrators

Locomotive manufacturers customarily lend new model diesels to prospective customers for extended use in the field. The reason is twofold: To work out the design bugs and to generate sales for the new models.

EMD built three demonstrator GP7s numbered 100, 200, and 300. Dressed in EMD's then-current colors of silver and dark blue with yellow trim, the demos tested on at least 14 Class I railroads, plus several terminal railroads. No. 100 demonstrated in the Upper Midwest on such roads as the Chicago & North Western, Milwaukee Road, and Soo Line. No. 200 took Horace Greeley's advice to "go west," where it worked in Salt Lake City for Union Pacific and hauled freight and passenger trains for Southern Pacific in the San Francisco Bay Area. As for No. 300, it went to work on Louisville & Nashville, Southern, and other railroads in the southeast.

◀ It wasn't the first road-switcher, but it turned out to be one of the most successful ones. Number 922 marks the world's first Geep, later renumbered No. 100. Electro-Motive photo

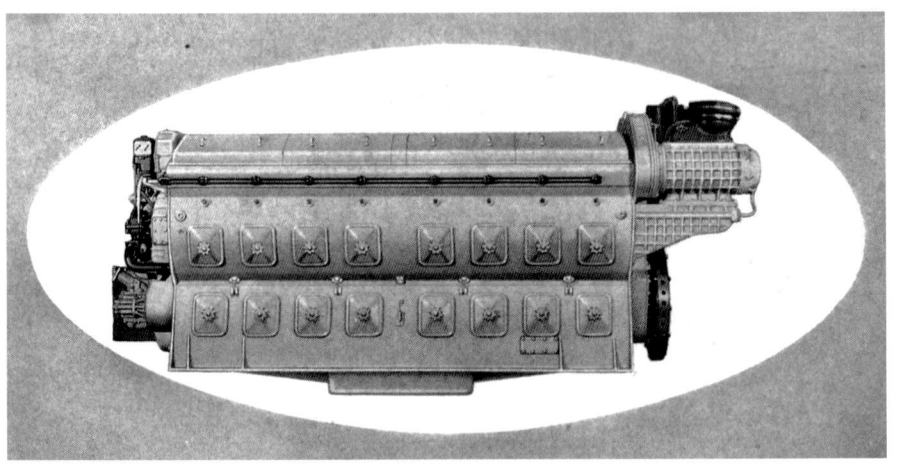

◀ "The General Motors GP-7 Diesel Road Switcher" sales brochure depicting a 16-567B prime mover.

▲ The airbrushed extra digit can't conceal the true identity of EMD 100, the first GP7. Both American Flyer and Atlas released models in this paint scheme. Electro-Motive photo

▶ EMD No. 300 stands on the Illinois Central main line at Brookhaven, Mississippi, in September 1950 after stalling on the grade. C. W. Witbeck photo

EMD Geeps, Model by Model

The GP7

Seventy-four railroads liked Dick Dilworth's "ugly duckling" GP7 enough to order 2,615 units, including 5 cabless units for Santa Fe. With or without a cab, a GP7 turns out 1,500 horsepower from a 16-cylinder 567B engine.

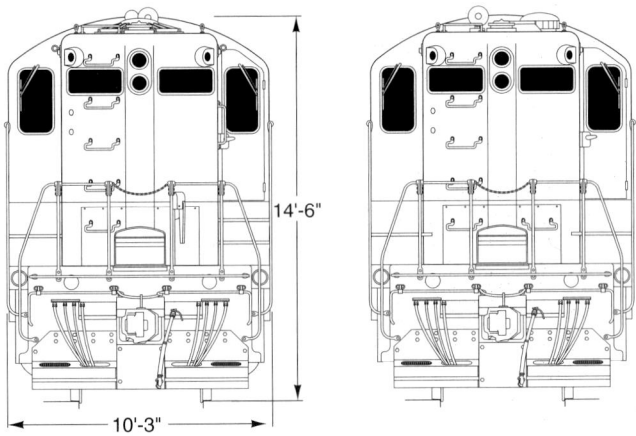

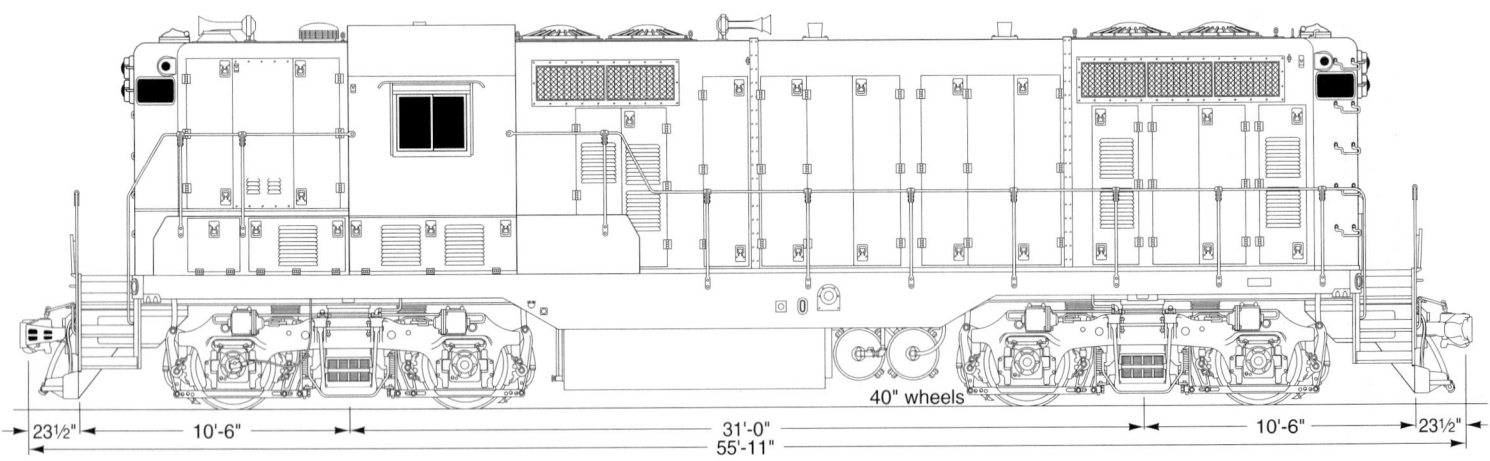

⬆ Great Northern 639 is a GP7, one of an order for 44 units built between 1950 and 1951. From October 1949 until August 1952 the GP7 had three sets of louvers below the cab and two vertical rows under the radiator shutters on the long hood. Norman Priebe photo

▲ The dynamic brake blister above the word "Lackawanna" on Delaware, Lackawanna & Western 952 disproves the once-common notion that only GP9s came with dynamic brakes. Two pairs of 36-inch fans on the roof provide engine cooling. Electro-Motive photo

⬆ Louisville & Nashville GP7 505 shows how EMD relocated the Geep's main air reservoirs to the top of the hood to allow for larger fuel and water tanks. Electro-Motive photo

▲ U.S. Army 1826 rides on optional AAR Type A switcher trucks. A dozen similar units wound up on the federally owned Alaska Railroad, which retrucked them with Type B road trucks from scrapped Alco RS-1s. Electro-Motive photo

The GP9

Introduction of the 567C engine brought about the 1,750-horsepower GP9, of which 3,601 units were built (including cabless units) between January 1954 and December 1959.

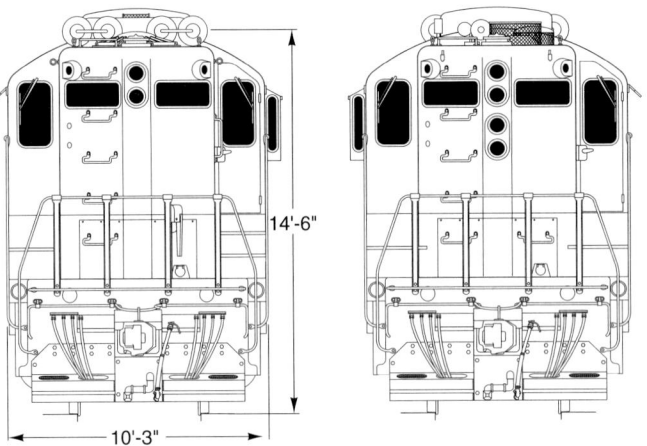

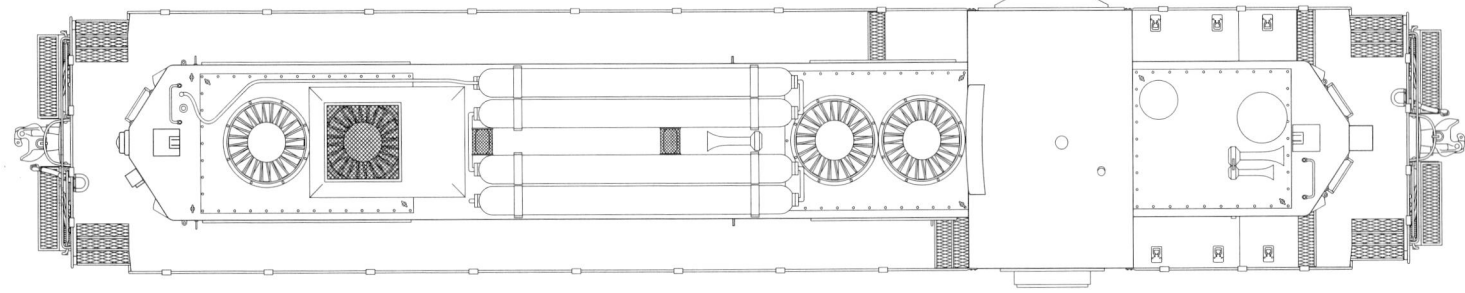

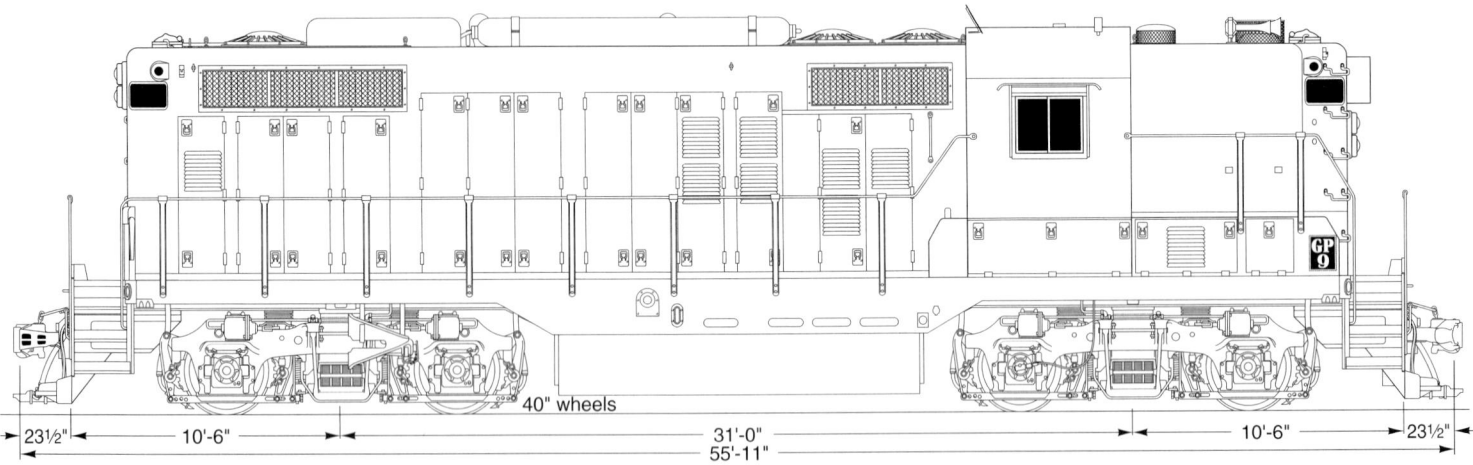

▶ Grand Trunk Western 1754 is an early-model GP9 with one set of louvers under the cab, one square set of louvers under the radiator shutters, and four uneven vertical rows of louvers on the long hood behind the cab. Electro-Motive photo

▶ Northern Pacific 376 is a late-model GP9 built in 1958. The single 48-inch cooling fan on the roof behind the cab distinguishes it from earlier Geeps. A boxy winterization hatch returns warm air to the interior of the long hood. Russell Schweizer photo

▶ Union Pacific 326B is one of 125 late-model GP9Bs delivered to UP (the Pennsylvania Railroad took 50, too). Cabless Geeps cost less to buy and saved on cab maintenance costs. However, the lack of a cab limited where the unit could be placed in a power consist, the main reason cabless units lost favor in the 1960s and 1970s. Electro-Motive photo

▶ Southern Pacific 3726 emerged from EMD in September 1959 with an optional EMD "low nose." The tapered low hood offered better forward visibility and appeared on many GP18s and subsequent models. George A. Trager photo

◀ Chicago & North Western GP9 No. 1714 contains two auxiliary lighting generators for Chicago-area suburban service. At the request of the Interstate Commerce Commission, EMD incorporated four fuel tank inspection holes in the sheet metal "skirts" over the fuel tanks on all Geeps built after 1952. Electro-Motive photo

◀ New York, New Haven & Hartford 1206 shows the third row of louvers added to the long hood behind the cab after January 1955. After June 1954 EMD switched from forged hand-rail stanchions to less expensive fabricated fittings. Electro-Motive photo

◀ Canadian National specified small fuel tanks (1,000 imperial gallon) and lightweight Flexicoil trucks for a number of Geeps destined for branchline service. EMD subsidiary General Motors Division of London, Ontario, staggered the spacing on the hood louvers to accommodate CN lettering. J. David Ingles photo

GP 18

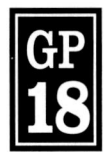

The GP18

It wasn't much, but a 50-horsepower boost from a 16-cylinder 567D1 engine launched the GP18, which totaled 350 sales between 1959 and 1963.

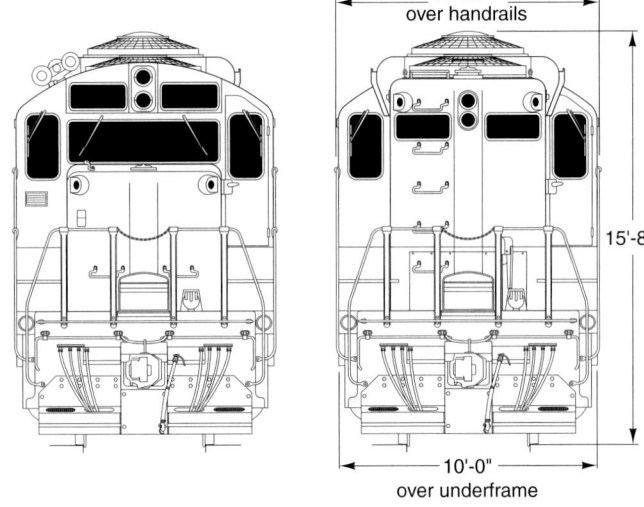

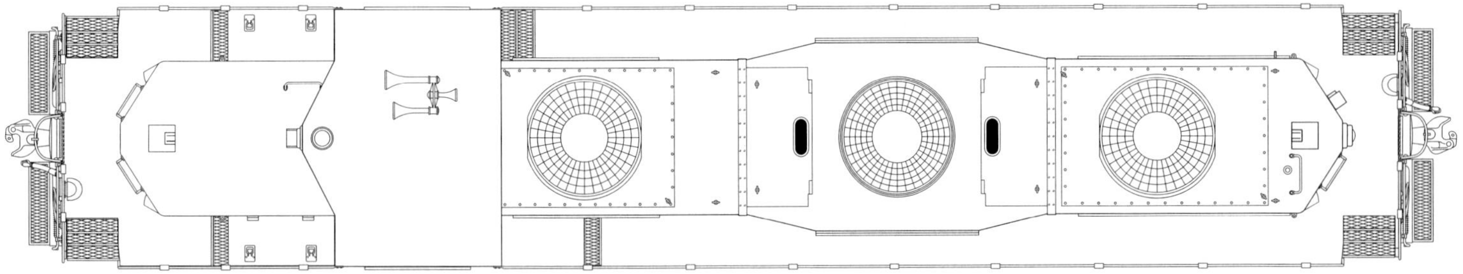

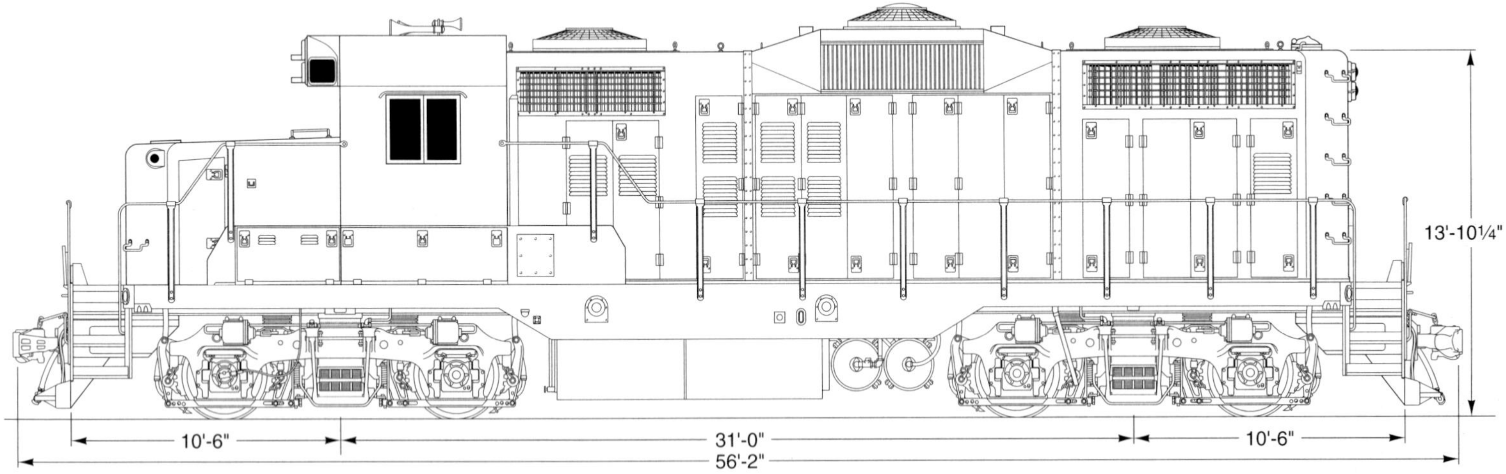

◂◂ Electro-Motive GP18 demonstrator 1800 (actually an airbrushed photo of a Rock Island unit) shows the fabricated metal grids over the radiator shutters on the long hood that replaced the earlier diagonal wire mesh or "chicken wire." EMD promised a 60 percent reduction in maintenance costs for GP18 buyers. Electro-Motive photo

◂ Boston & Maine 1770 represents the low-nose version of the GP18. EMD also used the one-piece cab windshield in the low-nose GP20. Expensive to replace when broken or damaged, it gave way to two-piece windshields in later-model EMD diesels, starting with 1961's GP30. Electro-Motive photo

◂ EMD's locomotive replacement program of the early 1960s allowed a railroad to trade in four old units on three equally productive new ones. At Missouri Pacific's request, EMD delivered 100 low-nose GP18s with Type B road trucks recycled from trade-in Alco FA cab units. Photo by Felix Brunot

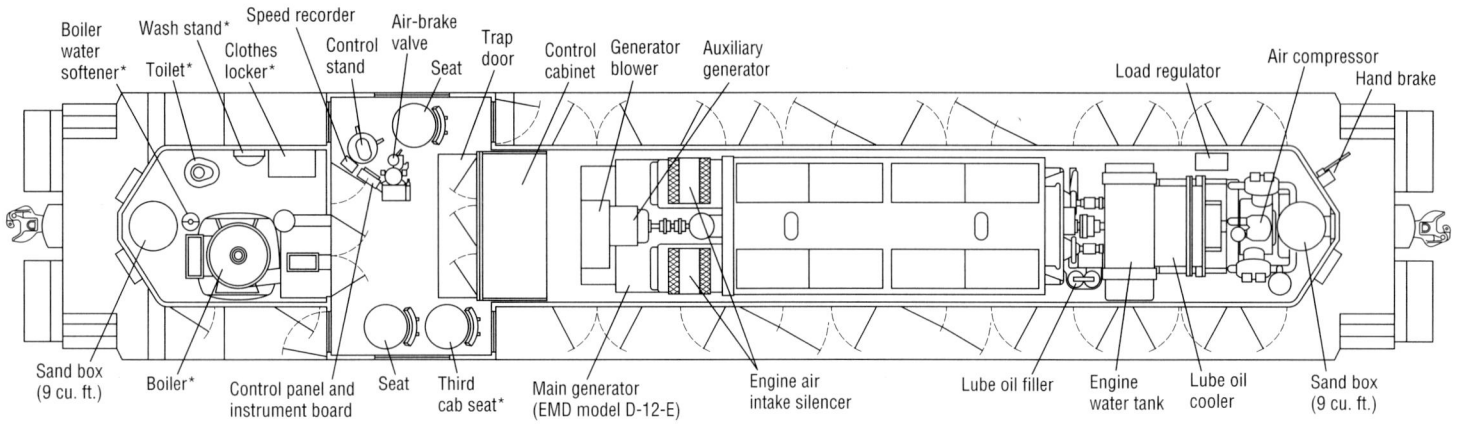
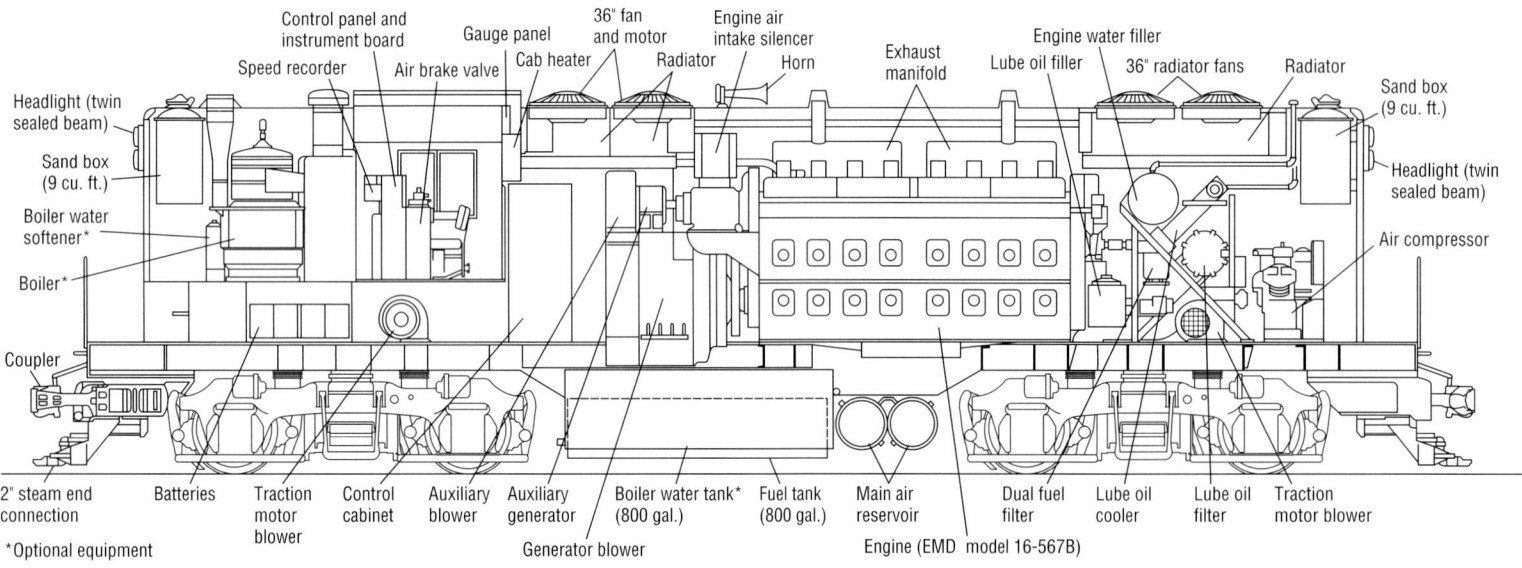

Have it your way: Geep factory options

Much of EMD's early success in the postwar diesel market came from its commitment to standardization. Unlike steam engines, which were typically custom-built for a particular railroad or region, most EMD diesels were sold "off the shelf."

Nonetheless, the builder offered the GP model line with several customer options, namely:

Fuel and water capacity

For trains operating long distances between service stops, EMD offered greater fuel and water capacity by relocating the Geep's main air reservoirs to the top of the long hood to make room for larger fuel and water tanks.

Passenger service

The Geep short hood offered room for a steam generator with 2,500-pound capacity (a boiler to furnish steam for heating passenger cars) and an 800-gallon water supply. Some Geeps built for commuter-train service came with two auxiliary generators hidden under a bulge in the end of the long hood.

Increased braking capacity

For use on steep grades EMD offered dynamic braking. This option temporarily employs traction motors as generators and uses the resulting electromotive force to slow down the train.

Long-hood-forward operation

Although designed to operate short-hood forward for better forward visibility, many railroads, especially in the East, specified long-hood-forward operation to give crews greater protection in highway crossing accidents.

Low short hood (low nose)

Mining customer Phelps Dodge Corporation ordered its long-hood-forward GP9s with low short hoods. The low short hood enabled engine crews to see over the train during loading operations. Southern Pacific's last order of GP9s and half of the 350 GP18s built came with low short hoods. With the introduction of the GP20 in 1959, low short hoods became standard equipment.

Trucks

The GP7 came with the customer's choice of switcher or road trucks. While most Geeps came on EMD's Blomberg road trucks, six GP7s delivered to Nashville, Chattanooga & St. Louis and 20 delivered to the U.S. Army rolled out of the factory on Type A switcher trucks.

Geeps Hard at Work

▸ **Atlantic Coast Line** purple and silver GP7 261 leads northbound freight No. 92 as it starts down a steep grade five miles south of Spartanburg, South Carolina, on June 29, 1960. ACL owned 212 GP7s but no GP9s. J. Parker Lamb photo

▸▸ Sporting a factory-option low nose, **Aberdeen & Rockfish's** lone GP18, painted blue and silver, leads a freight from Aberdeen to Fayetteville, North Carolina, in August 1965. The short line also owned one GP7. J. Parker Lamb photo

◀ Running backwards (normal operation was short-hood forward), **Santa Fe** GP7 2691 helps a 2-10-2 on Extra 3889 East over Cajon Pass in southern California. Shoving on the rear of the train is a four-unit set of EMD FT cab units. Stan Kistler photo

▲ Santa Fe GP7 2791 (which has a cab) sits with its stablemate, GP7B 2791A (which does not). The railroad owned 250 GP7s (including five cabless versions) and 52 GP9s. Santa Fe Railway photo

▶ A Santa Fe piggyback train rolls out of Oakland headed for nearby Richmond, California, behind GP7 2812, one of a group of 52 units built in 1952. Santa Fe skipped the GP18, then purchased 75 low-nose GP20s. Richard Steinheimer photo

▶▶ Three **Bangor & Aroostook** blue and gray GP7s (leased to the Pennsylvania Railroad) watch a westbound New York Central freight pass Cleveland's Municipal Stadium behind a GP9 and two EMD cab units in June 1961. Herbert H. Harwood photo

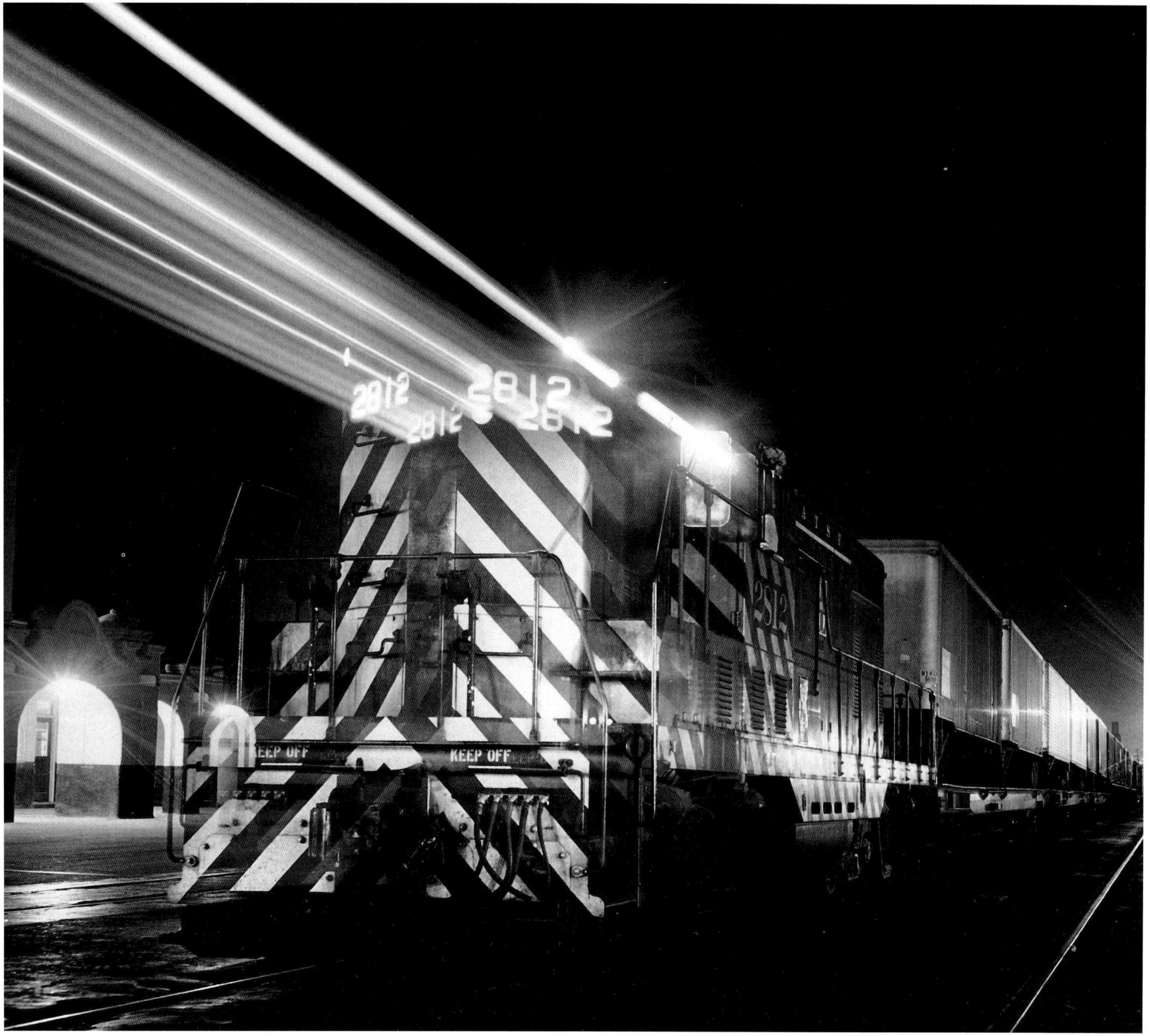

◀◀ Two blue **Baltimore & Ohio** GP9s lend their combined 3,500 horsepower to a steam-powered eastbound ore train near Akron, Ohio, on July 22, 1957. B&O had 32 GP7s, 194 GP9s, and one (yes, one) GP18. Herbert H. Harwood Jr. photo

◀ B&O GP9 3414 speeds the northbound *Cincinnatian* near Dayton, Ohio, on March 9, 1957. Geeps with roof-mounted air reservoirs were often called "torpedo-boat" Geeps. J. Parker Lamb photo

▲ **Belt Railway of Chicago** GP7 470, painted gray and black, shoves loaded coal cars at the Rail to Water bulk loading facility on the south side of Chicago. Geeps were the exception to the switchers used by other Chicago-area terminal roads. John Gruber photo

▶ **Boston & Maine** train MP-3 crosses the Hudson River at Mechanicville, New York. A low-nose GP18 leads three B&M GP9s with high short hoods. Jim Shaughnessy photo

▶ Three of Boston & Maine's 50 GP9s pose at the railroad's yard in Mechanicville, N.Y., in March 1958. B&M's GP9s, called "Bluebirds" for their color, were delivered with dynamic brakes. Jim Shaughnessy photo

▶▶ **Chicago, Burlington & Quincy** train No. 72 thunders through Spanish Lake, Missouri, behind GP7s 262 and 273. A loyal EMD road-switcher customer, the "Q" went for 68 GP7s and 20 GP9s painted black and gray with red and yellow striping. John C. Illman photo

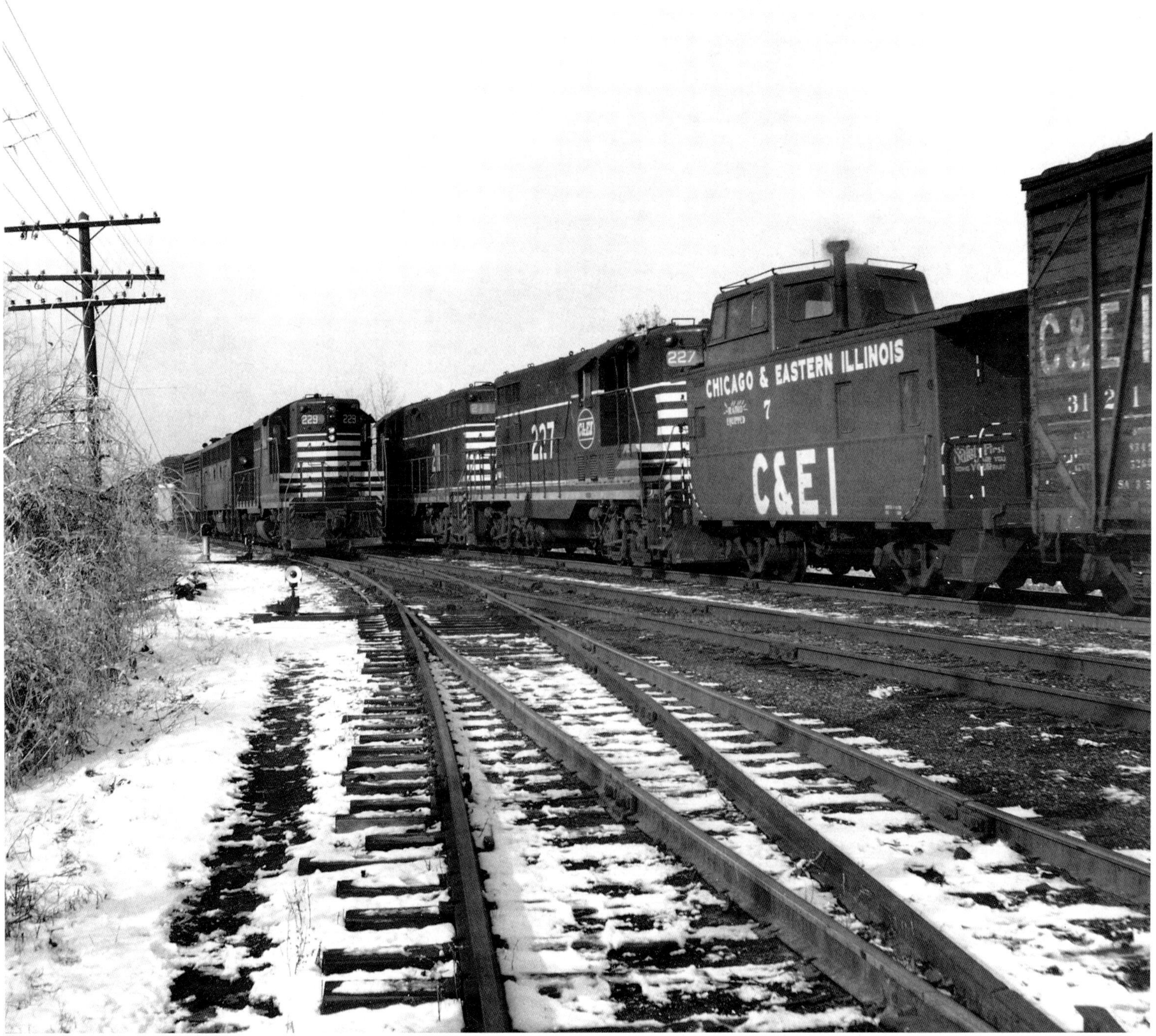

◂◂ **Central of Georgia** GP9 166 leads three Alco RS-3s on the point of a northbound freight at Weems, Alabama, on July 4, 1959. The Savannah, Georgia–based railroad owned 15 GP7s, 11 GP9s, and 8 GP18s, all delivered in blue and gray with yellow trim. J. Parker Lamb photo

◂ Geeps meet Geeps as **Chicago & Eastern Illinois** GP7 229, leading two F units, meets the Villa Grove local at Danville, Illinois, on December 23, 1958. J. Parker Lamb photo

◄ Known to some railfans as "torpedo boats," two GP9s with roof-mounted air reservoirs lead eastbound **Milwaukee Road** train No. 18 through the Lake Chatcolet country of northern Idaho. Joseph Sweeney photo

▲ Steam-generator-equipped orange and black GP9s 204 and 208 have arrived on a Chicago, Milwaukee, St Paul & Pacific commuter train in Elgin, Illinois. The Milwaukee Road owned 128 GP9s but no GP7s or GP18s. C. S. Mote photo

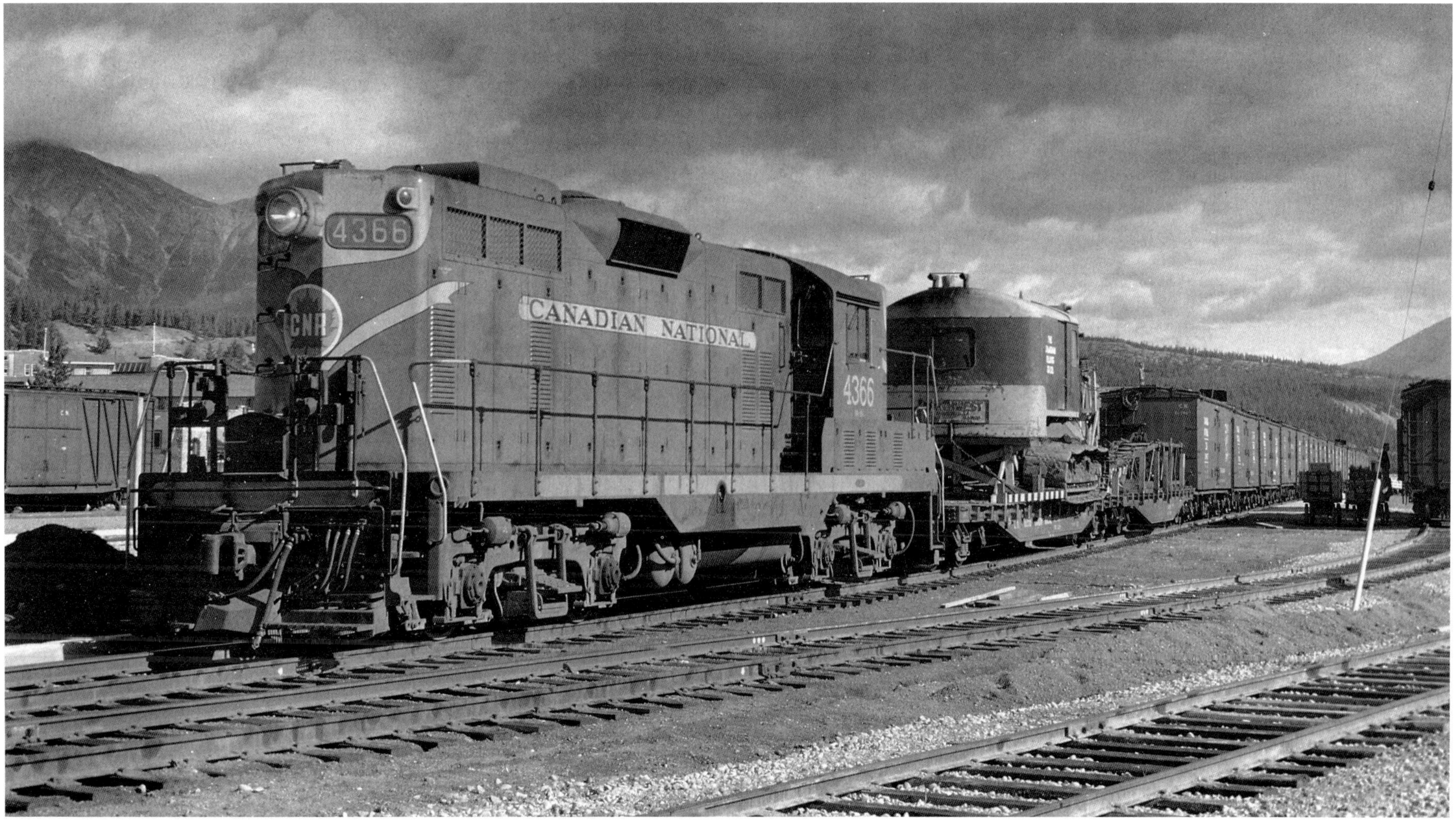

◀ Westbound Milwaukee Road freight 263 rolls over a high trestle between St. Maries and Malden, Idaho, in May 1964. Sixty Milwaukee Road GP9s built between June 1954 and July 1959 came with dynamic brakes. Richard Steinheimer photo

▲ **Canadian National** GP7 4366 at Jasper, Alberta, sorts cars for train 391, the twice-weekly mixed train to Blue River, British Columbia, on August 13, 1957. EMD's Canadian subsidiary GMD built 25 GP7s and 349 GP9s for CN. John C. Illman photo

▶ While 2-8-0 No. 470 looks on from the siding, olive green Canadian National GP7 4370 leads two Geeps and 48 cars north on CN subsidiary Central Vermont's main line at Amherst, Massachusetts. CV proper owned 18 GP9s. David Plowden photo

▶▶ The skyline of lower Manhattan frames a switchman standing on a boxcar coupled to the rear of dark green **Central of New Jersey** GP7 1526 at Jersey City, N.J. CNJ owned 13 GP7s (all with generators for commuter train service) and 2 GP9s. David Plowden photo

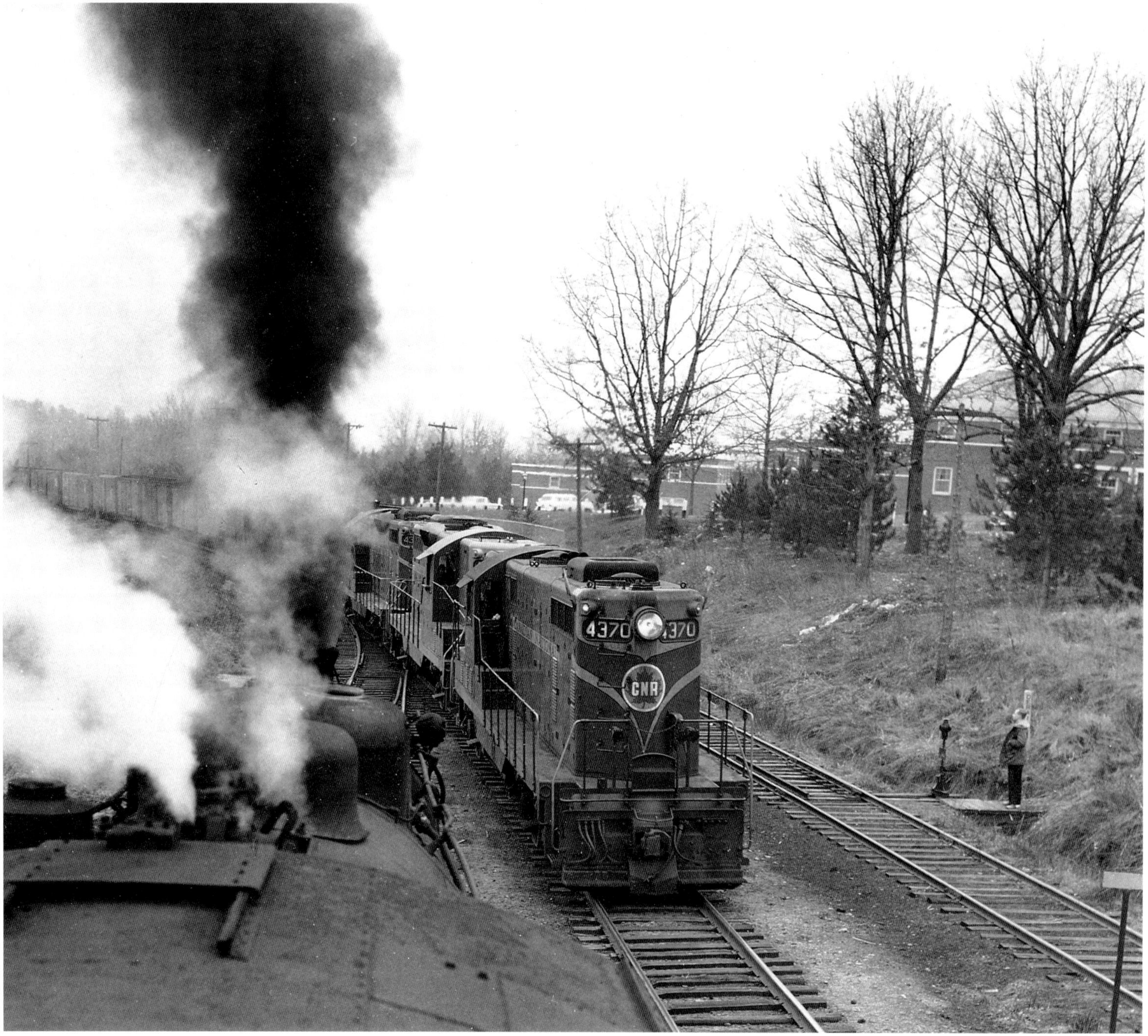

◂◂ Dynamic-brake-equipped GP9s supplemented **Canadian Pacific**'s fleet of aging Fairbanks-Morse diesels in southern Alberta and British Columbia in the 1960s. CP owned 17 GP7s and 200 GP9s, delivered in maroon and gray. Mike Schafer photo

◂ Three **Chicago & North Western** GP9s and a lone Alco roadswitcher hoist time freight Number 380 up Radnor Hill, north of Peoria, Illinois, on October 3, 1960. The trailing unit is an Alco RS3 rebuilt by the builder with a 251 engine and an RS11 long hood. J. Parker Lamb photo

▶ Four of C&NW's 124 GP7s stand next to a string of retired steam engines at Proviso Yard near Chicago in 1956. C&NW photo

▶▶ Commuters gawk at C&NW No. 1520, tangible proof of North Western's decision to dieselize its Chicago-area commuter service on Friday, May 11, 1956. Besides GP7s, North Western owned 59 GP9s and 6 GP18s. No. 1520 is the former EMD demonstrator 300 (page 11). All C&NW Geeps were yellow and green. C&NW photo

▲ **Chesapeake & Ohio** bought 193 GP7s from EMD, including the 6 visible in this photo, to dieselize former Pere Marquette Lines in Michigan. C&O 5747 is one of 59 units built between October 1951 and January 1952. David P. Morgan Library Collection

▶ C&O sprang for 363 GP9s, including these three solid dark blue examples equipped with dynamic brakes. Unlike rival coal-hauler Norfolk & Western, C&O preferred to run its Geeps short-hood forward, which explains the bell on the roof of the short hood. C&O photo

▶ With a main line that crossed the Rocky Mountains between Denver, Colorado, and Salt Lake City, Utah, it's no surprise **Denver & Rio Grande Western** ordered its 24 GP9s with dynamic brakes. "The Grande," as it was known, also owned 14 similarly equipped GP7s. Robert Hale photo

▶▶ Framed by Utah's Wasatch Mountains in the background, D&RGW GP9 5912 tows the Burgin Mine train along the Tintic Branch in April 1966. D&RGW's black and gold Geeps were set up for short-hood-forward operation. Richard Steinheimer photo

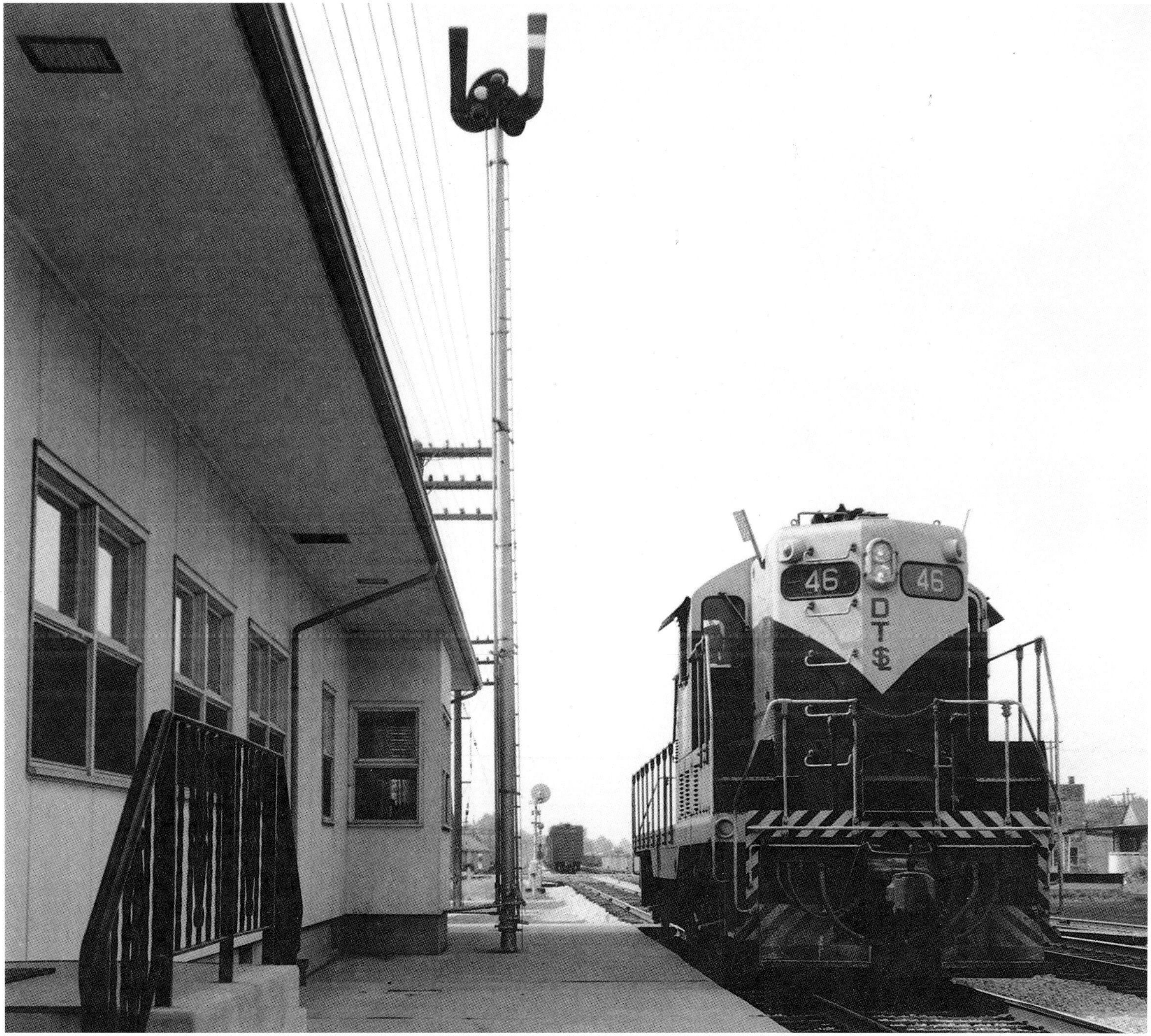

◀◀ **Detroit, Toledo & Ironton's** "Rouge Puller" bangs across the Wabash main at Oakwood Junction, Michigan, on August 16, 1959. Up front is orange GP7 957, one of 24 such units on the roster. The concrete arches above the train are remnants of DT&I's 1920-era electrification. J. David Ingles photo

◀ **Detroit & Toledo Shore Line** No. 46 at Monroe, Michigan, is one of 10 blue and yellow GP7s built for D&TSL between January 1951 and February 1953. Philip Hastings photo

D. & T.S.L.

▶ A locomotive hostler at Secaucus, New Jersey, checks the sand level on Erie 1241, one of 23 black and yellow GP7s built for the railroad between March 1951 and September 1952. Erie also owned six GP9s. Henry J. Ehlbeck photo

▶▶ **Erie Lackawanna** GP7 1400—still wearing Erie Railroad colors—leads a westbound commuter train past Paterson, New Jersey, on January 29, 1964. Erie contributed 52 GP7s to the 20 owned by merger partner Delaware, Lackawanna & Western. William S. Young photo

▸ Two EL GP7s in maroon and gray lead four Alco RS-3s past SF Tower in Suffern, New York, in July 1967. The Alcos use four-cycle turbocharged engines rated at 1,600 horsepower versus two-cycle nonturbocharged engines in the Geeps. Philip D. Francis photo

▸▸ **St Louis-San Francisco** Geeps tie onto a freight on subsidiary Quanah, Acme & Pacific delivered by the Santa Fe at Floydada, Texas. Known as the Frisco, SLSF owned 128 black PGP7s but no GP9s. Donald Sims photo

▶ Led by black GP7 522, Frisco freight No. 730 blasts through an early winter snowstorm at Nichols, Missouri, on New Year's Eve, 1967. The second Geep wears Frisco's Mandarin orange and white colors, inspired by the paint scheme on EMD's GP35/DD35 demonstrators (built in 1963). Clyde L. Anderson photo

▶▶ Framed by the concrete coal tower at Camak, Georgia, blue and silver GP9 1040 of the Georgia Railroad leads freight No. 209 between Augusta and Atlanta, Ga. The railroad owned 16 GP7s and 3 GP9s. Victor Hand photo

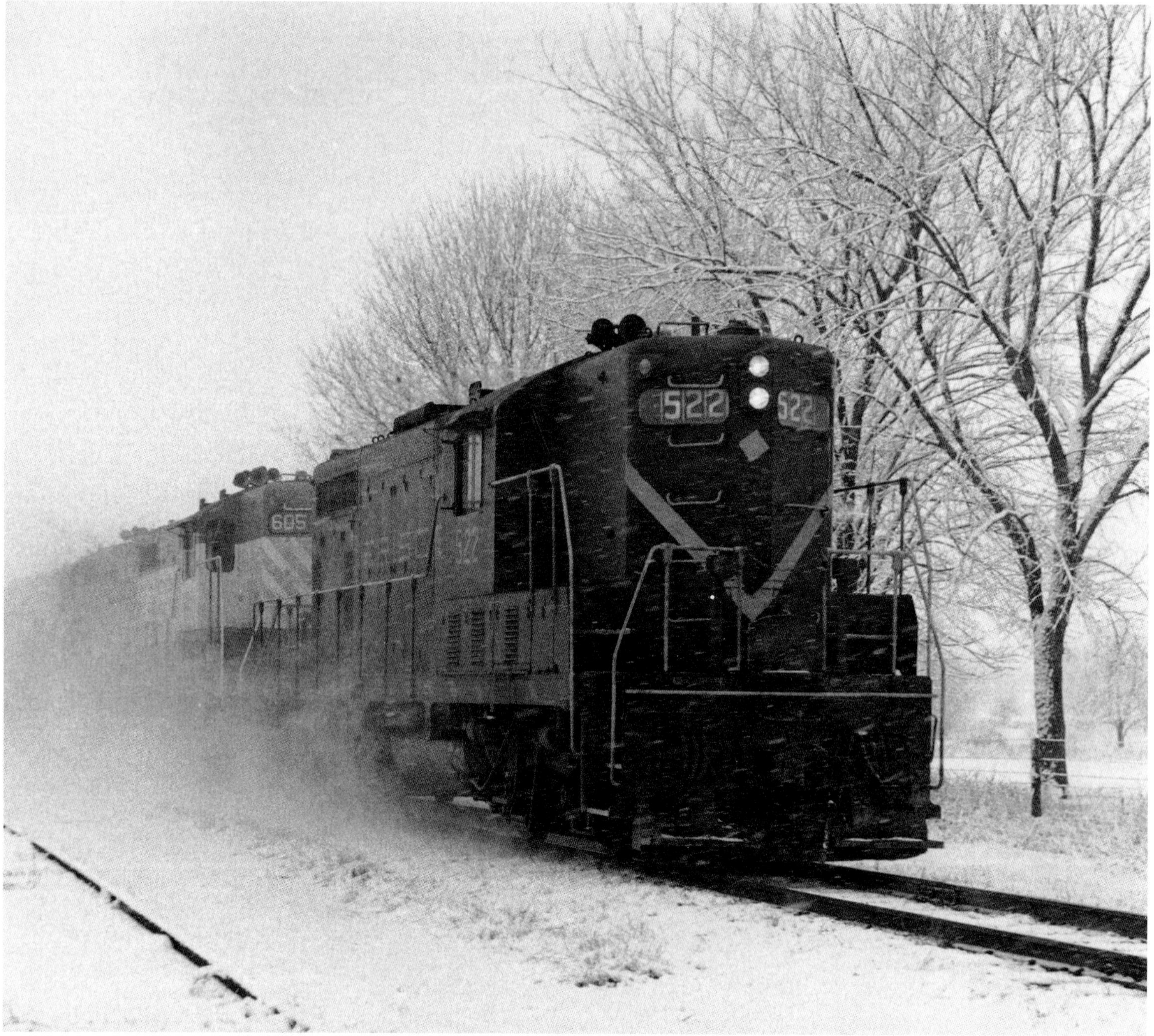

▸ So new you can smell the olive green and yellow paint, a string of **Grand Trunk Western** GP9s poses at EMD's McCook, Illinois, factory with the road name emblazoned on the side sills, but with the nose emblems not yet applied. GTW owned 51 GP9s and 11 GP18s, but no GP7s. Electro-Motive photo

▸▸ Eastbound local No. 576 and westbound time-freight No. 417 meet at Marshall, Minnesota, on **Great Northern**'s Wilmar Division in August 1961. GN embraced the Geep to the tune of 56 GP7s and 95 GP9s, all painted orange and dark green. Norman Priebe photo

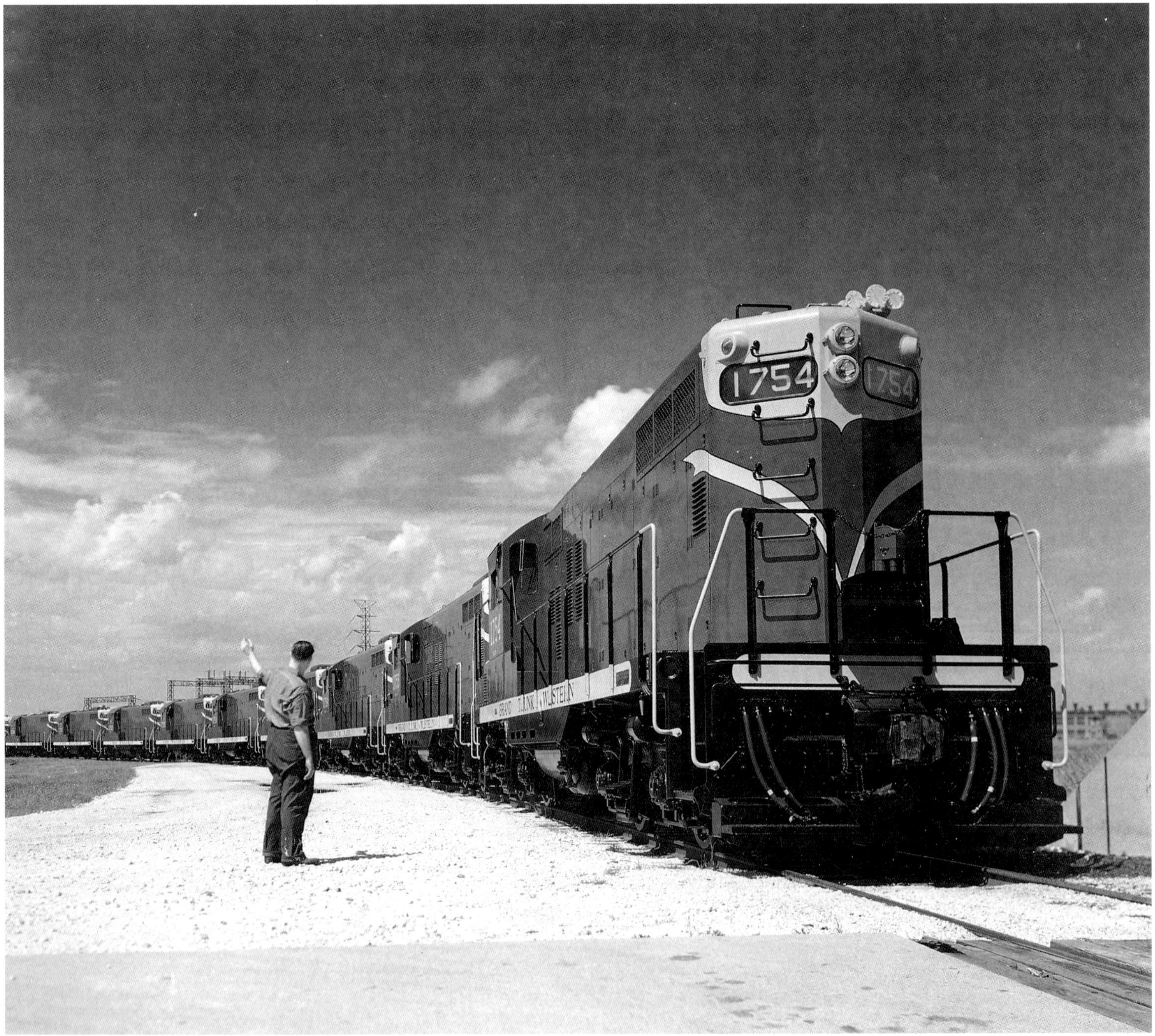

◀ Three GP9s and a lone GP7 lean into the rear of Great Northern train No. 492 near Columbia Falls, Montana, on February 27, 1968. Only the GP7 (the unit coupled to the caboose) lacks dynamic brakes. Edward Kanak photo

▲ Four GP9s shove on the rear of a Great Northern freight on Marias Pass in Montana on May 1964. GN, the only big western road to set up its Geeps as long-hood forward, went on to order 36 GP20s, all with high short hoods and dynamic brakes. Richard Steinheimer photo

▶ Watched by a pair of Kansas City Southern EMD E8s on the *Southern Belle,* **Illinois Central** GP7 8800 leads the *Northeastern Limited* out of Shreveport, Louisiana, on August 7, 1964. Roof-mounted air reservoirs point to the Geep's large-capacity water and fuel tanks. J. Parker Lamb photo

▶▶ Powered by three black GP9s, IC train CC-6 waits for a green signal at Fort Dodge, Iowa, on October 12, 1967. Shown on the timecard as train No. 76, this was the so-called "meat train" between Council Bluffs, Iowa, and Chicago. William D. Middleton photo

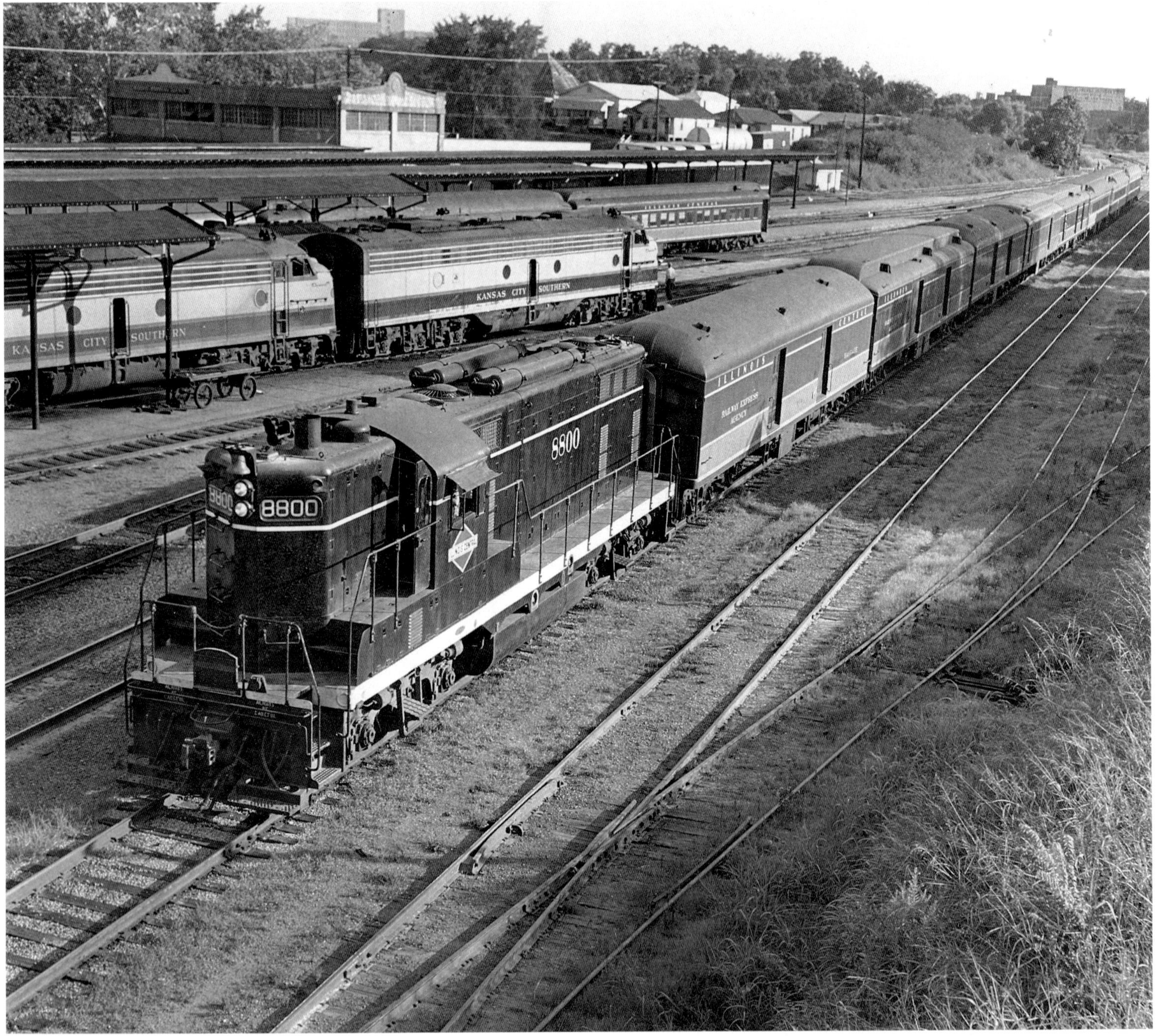

◀◀ Illinois Central's eastbound *Land O' Corn* streamliner glides past GP9 9109 leading IC's "meat train" at Freeport, Illinois, on October 12, 1957. IC stuck with nonturbocharged EMD power until it acquired 3,000-horsepower GP40s in the late 1960s. William D. Middleton photo

◀ Geeps meet Geeps on the Illinois Central Iowa Division main along the Mississippi River at Dubuque, Iowa. A loyal EMD customer, IC bought 48 GP7s, 348 GP9s, and 29 GP18s. William D. Middleton photo

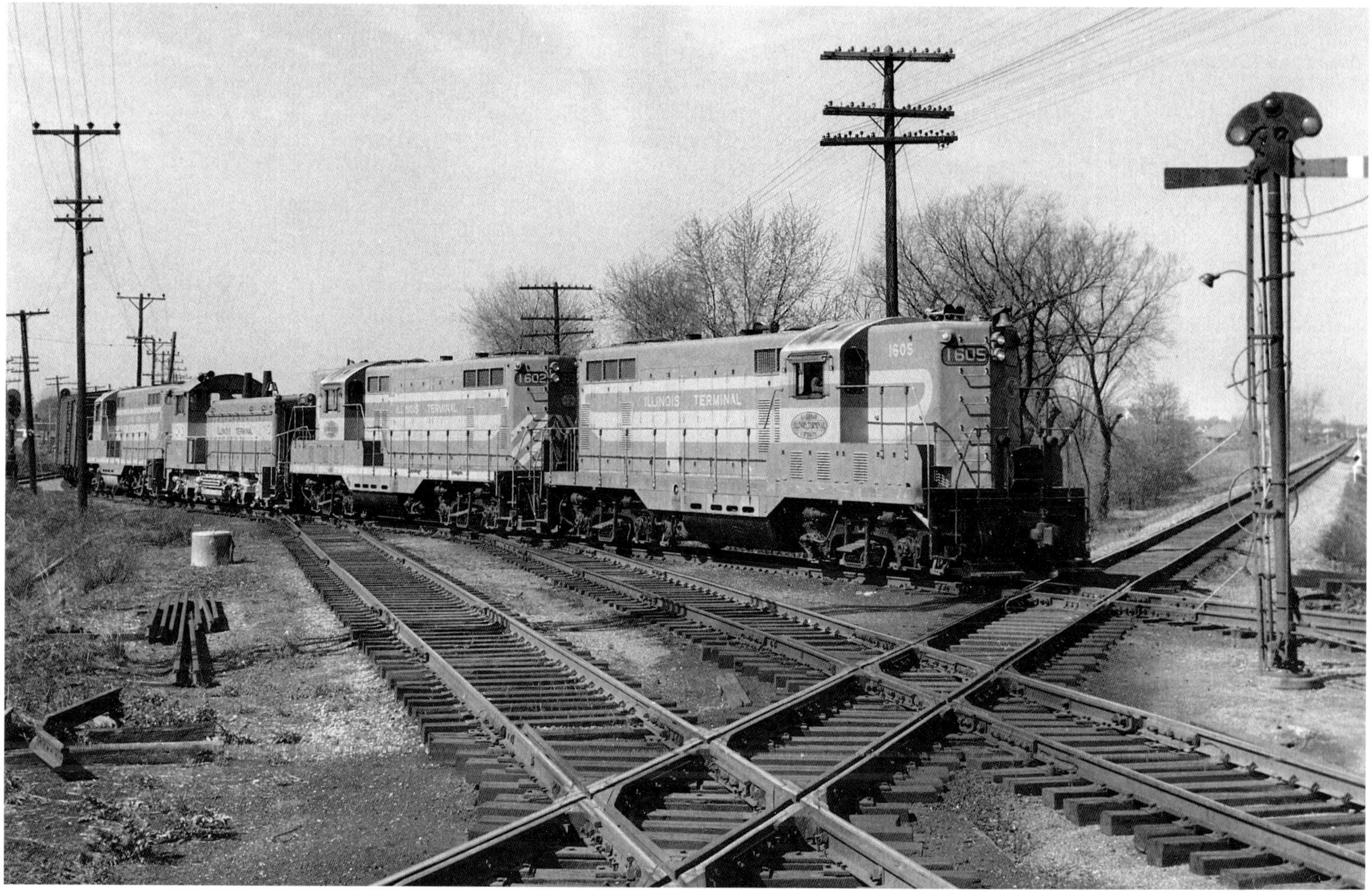

◄ **Illinois Terminal** freight No. 202 leaves the Edwardsville, Illinois, yard for East Peoria behind lime green and yellow GP7s 1605 and 1604 on January 25, 1955. Diesels replaced steam and electric locomotives on the IT, a former interurban railroad based in St. Louis, Missouri. William D. Middleton photo

▲ An EMD switcher on Flexicoil road trucks splices three IT Geeps headed north across the Illinois Central and Wabash diamonds at Starnes, Illinois, in the state capital city of Springfield. IT's Geep fleet totaled six GP7s built in March and August of 1953. Walter A. Peters photo

▶ Headed for Birmingham, Alabama, **Louisville & Nashville** GP7s 422 and 433 lead a freight across U.S. Highways 82 and 43 and past the L&N passenger station at Tuscaloosa, Alabama, on November 6, 1955. Hayden T. Alford photo

◀ Powered by passenger-service GP7 550, a one-car L&N local clatters over the Pascagoula River at the Mississippi town of the same name on December 29, 1958. Nicknamed the "Old Reliable," L&N owned 59 GP7s and 30 GP9s painted dark blue and yellow with orange trim. J. Parker Lamb photo

◀◀ **Louisville & Nashville** touted its five GP18s as replacements for 29 older diesels. The new units arrived on the property between June and July of 1960 sporting L&N's new gray and yellow colors and factory low noses, complete with nose-mounted headlights for increased grade crossing visibility. Louisville & Nashville photo

◀ **Lehigh Valley** GP18 No. 303 takes on fuel and sand at the company's Sayre, Pennsylvania, engine terminal in June 1964. Favoring early Alco road-switchers over comparable EMDs, LV owned just six Geeps: two GP9s and four high-nose GP18s, all painted Cornell red. William J. Brennan photo

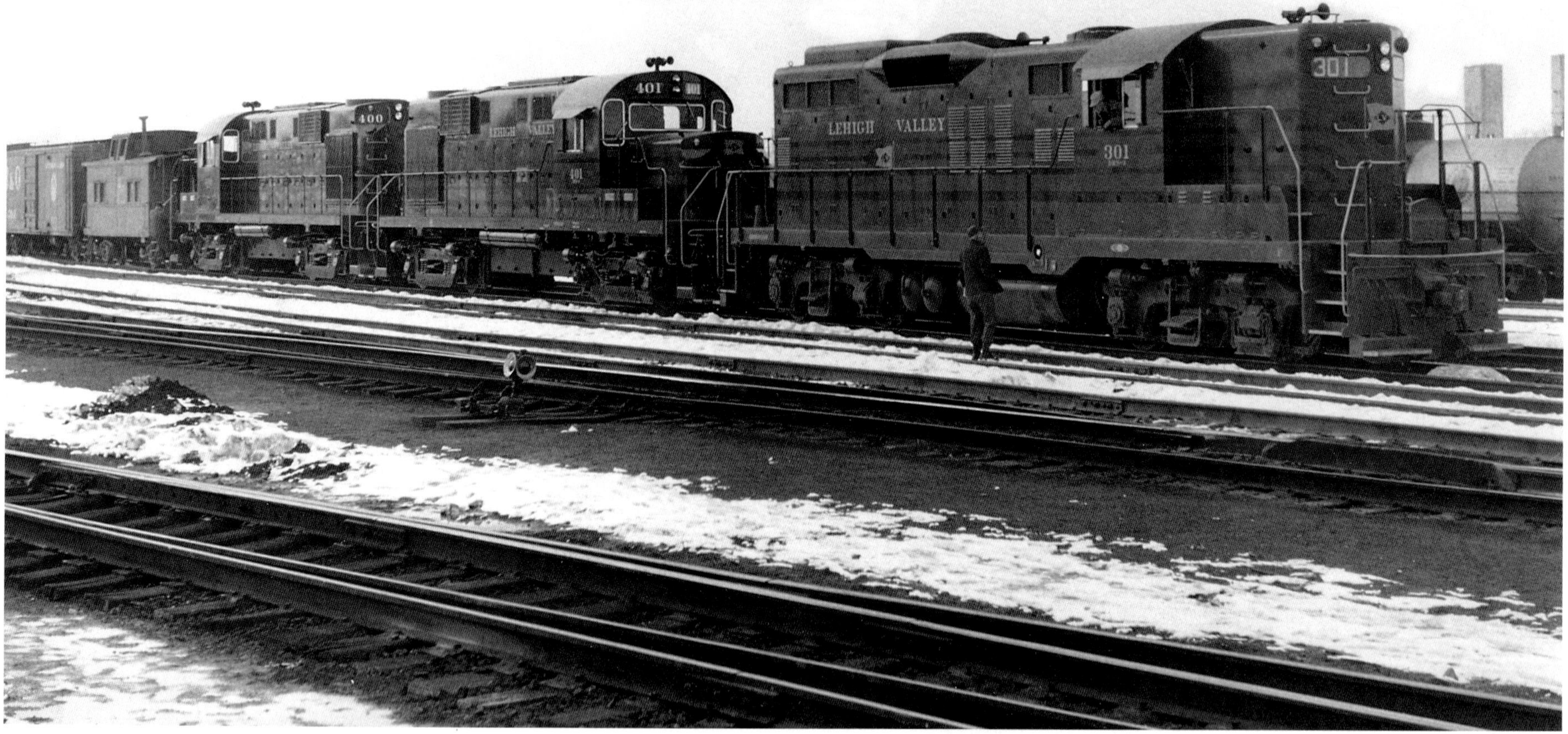

▲ One half of Lehigh Valley's GP9 fleet teams up with two 1,800-horsepower RS-11 locomotives built by EMD competitor Alco. All LV Geeps came with dynamic brakes. Carl Rogoza photo

▶ Three **Maine Central** GP7s lead an F3A and 89 cars up the 2.35 percent grade of Crawford Notch, New Hampshire, on August 3, 1966. MEC owned 19 GP7s, nine of which came with dynamic brakes like the three shown here. Jim Shaughnessy photo

▲ All by itself, **Missouri-Kansas-Texas** red GP7 1512 moves a northbound freight through Caddo Mills, Texas, on September 3, 1952. The "Katy" took 33 GP7s but passed on the GP9 and GP18. R. S. Plummer photo

▶ **Missouri Pacific** GP7 4149 leads two Alco cab units and 109 cars south out of Omaha, Nebraska, bound for Kansas City in February 1959. In steam days the "Mop" used its heaviest 2-10-2 steam engines on this roller-coaster line north of Kansas City. Thomas O. Dutch photo

▲ One of Missouri Pacific's 229 blue and gray GP7s powers the local freight between McGehee and La Grange, Arkansas, in July 1957. MP also owned 54 GP9s and 151 GP18s. Johnnie M. Gray photo

◀ Two passenger cars barely tax the capability of GP7 4321, seen leading Missouri Pacific's Pleasant Hill passenger train on White River Line across Bear Creek north of Bergman, Arkansas, on June 8, 1960. Betty Love photo

◀ **Minneapolis & St. Louis** owned 23 red and white GP9s, including No. 706 (with dynamic brakes) leading Illinois Central GP9 (without dynamic brakes) on a run-through freight across Iowa in July 1960. Don Hofsommer photo

▲ Working as helpers, two maroon and yellow **Nashville, Chattanooga & St. Louis** GP7s lead the *Dixie Flyer* and its two F units downgrade into Cowan, Tennessee, in April 1951. NC&StL owned 37 GP7s. A. C. Kalmbach photo

▶ **Phelps-Dodge Corporation** GP9 21, EMD's first low-nose Geep, shoves copper ore at a mine in Arizona. The company's 17 gray GP9s had nonsloping noses, wheel bearing guards (on the trucks), 800-gallon fuel tanks, and extra engine air filters (on the long hood behind the cab). Donald Sims photo

▶▶ **New York Central** two-tone gray GP9 5963 leads a black and gray F7A on a westbound freight through Berea, Ohio, on January 17, 1957. NYC signed up for 176 GP9s, including a dozen units built in Canada by GMD. Herbert H. Harwood Jr. photo

▲ Peoria & Eastern GP7s 5621 and 5622 roll west at Champaign, Illinois, on October 17, 1953. A subsidiary of New York Central, P&E operated between Peoria, Bloomington, and Danville, Illinois, and Indianapolis, Indiana. G. E. Lloyd photo

◄ A Gulf, Mobile & Ohio E7A on the northbound *Abraham Lincoln* looks on during refueling as New York Central GP9 5979 and three sister Geeps back up to tie onto their Peoria & Eastern train at Bloomington, Illinois, on August 15, 1959. Bruce R. Meyer photo

▶ In 1951 EMD subsidiary GMD of London, Ontario, built 19 GP7s for Chesapeake & Ohio service in Canada. When C&O canceled the order, the Geeps went to New York Central. Still wearing C&O blue and yellow colors (but NYC numbers), 5827 sits at St. Thomas, Ontario, on November 8, 1956. Herbert H. Harwood photo

▶▶ Peoria & Eastern GP7 5625 waits as a truck unloads express business at Peoria Union Station on March 10, 1958. In total, 14 of New York Central's 169 GP7s were lettered for P&E, including two with steam generators. Fred Scott photo

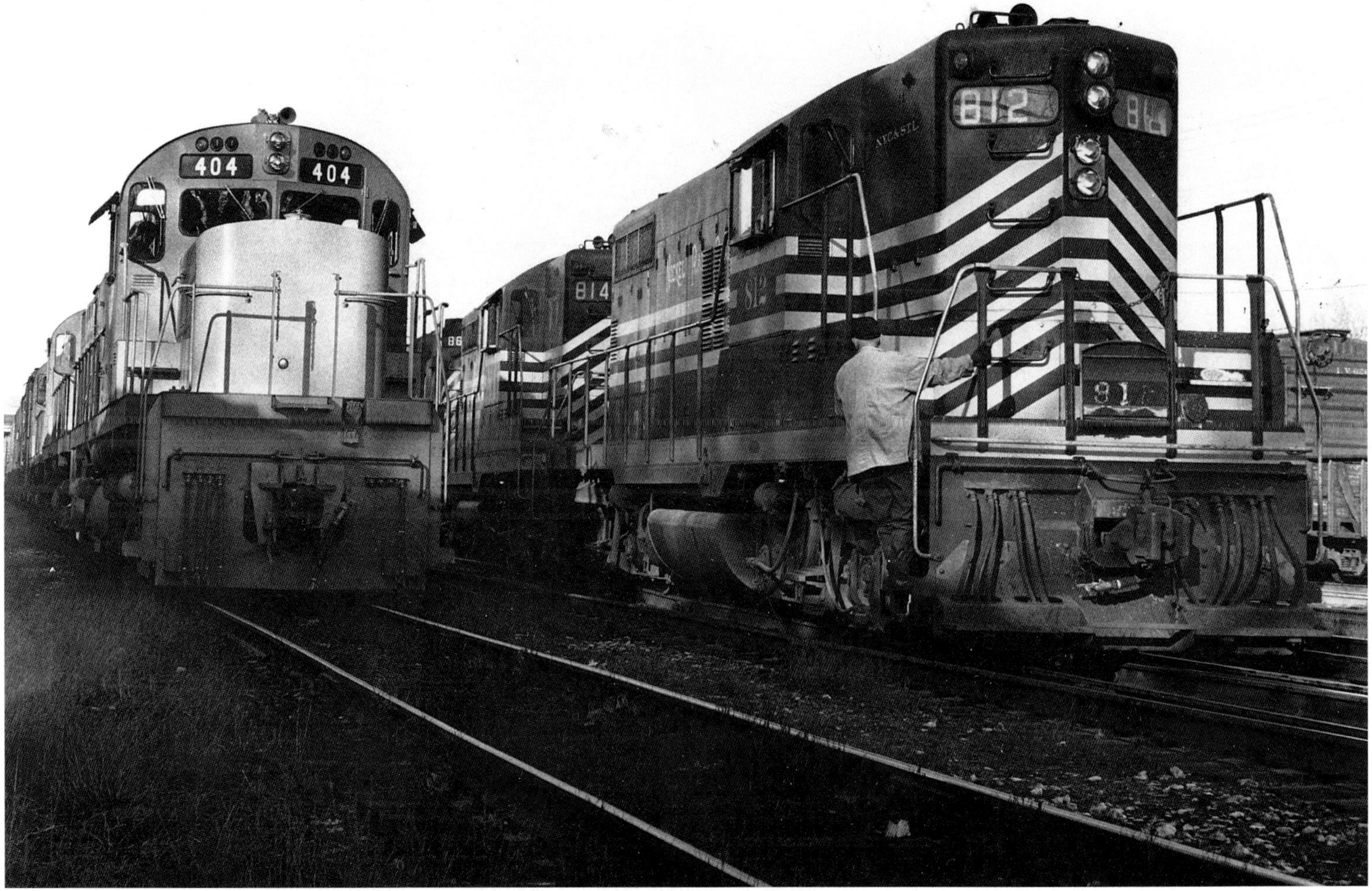

◀◀ A GP9 belonging to the **New York, Chicago & St. Louis** (known as the Nickel Plate) leads a run-through freight (operated jointly with the Lehigh Valley) through Odessa, New York, on January 5, 1964. The Nickel Plate stabled 48 GP7s, 111 GP9s, and 10 GP18s. J. J. Young Jr. photo

◀ Nickel Plate 812 appears again at Sayre, Pennsylvania, handing off the jointly operated NKP-LV run-through freight to LV C-420 diesels built by Alco Products. J. J. Young Jr. photo

◀ Three Geeps lead Nickel Plate freight MB-98 (right) past train No. 45 at Ramsey, Illinois, on May 9, 1959. NKP 529 is the last of an order for 20 GP9s built in March 1958. J. Parker Lamb photo

▲ Nickel Plate GP9 520 trails a consist made up of Geeps and Alco RS-11s painted black with yellow striping on the point of train NC-3 at Cleveland, Ohio, in July 1959. Herbert H. Harwood Jr. photo

▶ **Norfolk & Western** GP9 711 leads two 1,800-horsepower Alco RS-11s south of Bluefield, Virginia, on August 28, 1957. During the 1940s and early 1950s, a ready source of good, inexpensive bituminous coal (the lion's share of N&W's traffic) and the efficiency of its steam engines caused the Roanoke, Virginia—based carrier to pass on early cab-unit diesels. EMD finally got its foot in the roundhouse door with 4 GP9s built in September 1955; N&W eventually ordered 306 GP9s. Bruce Meyer photo

▶▶ Merger with Nickel Plate and the Wabash in 1964 brought more Geeps to N&W's stable. A former Nickel Plate blue GP10, a freight unit, leads the St. Louis—bound *Banner Blue* (a former Wabash train) out of Chicago's Dearborn Station for the last time on September 9, 1967. Bob Clarkson photo

▶ In an airbrushed publicity photo, N&W's first four GP9s, dressed in solid black, lead a loaded coal train on the Norfolk Division near Bonsook, Virginia. GP7s didn't appear on N&W's locomotive roster until the railroad merged with the Nickel Plate and Wabash in 1964. N&W photo

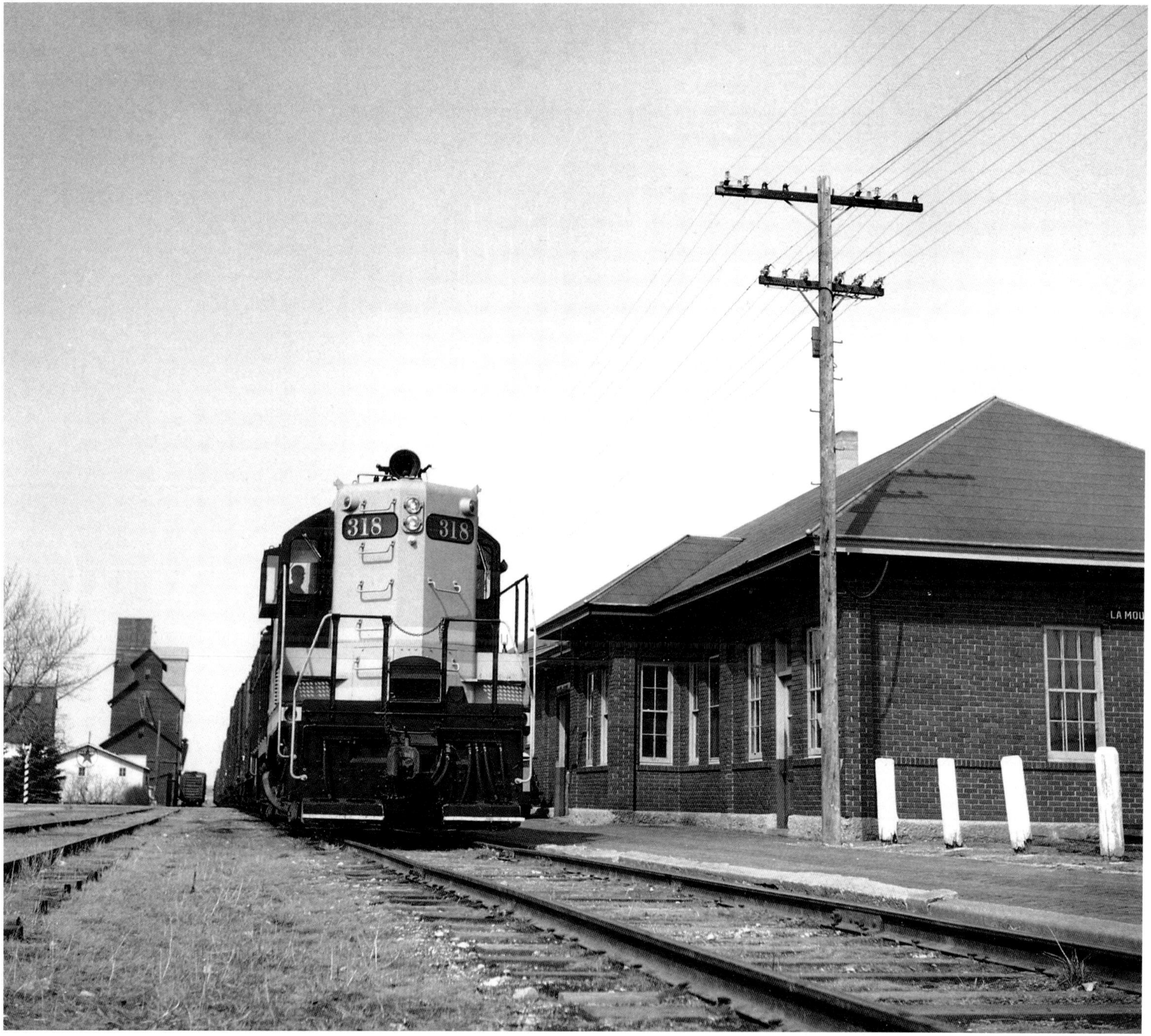

◀◀ On its way to Auburn from Sedro Woolley, Washington, **Northern Pacific** GP7 557 rolls through Kirkland in September 1952. NP owned 20 GP7s, including one unit (569) with a steam generator. Jim Fredrickson photo

◀ Northern Pacific mixed train No. 154, powered by GP9 318, arrives at LeMoure, North Dakota, on its daily-except-Sunday trip between Jamestown and Oakes on April 20, 1959. NP purchased 176 GP9s and 9 GP18s. William D. Middleton photo

◀ Fresh from EMD, **New York, Susquehanna & Western** GP18s (with low short hoods and dynamic brakes) pause at Erie Lackawanna's yard at Susquehanna, Pennsylvania, on September 3, 1962. Wearing an EMD-designed black and yellow scheme, these were the first (and only) Geeps for the "Susie-Q," which assigned only even numbers to diesels with m.u. capability. William S. Young photo

◂◂ Three **Pennsylvania** GP9s lead an eastbound train of refrigerated boxcars into Enola, Pennsylvania, in December 1955. The Pennsy owned 66 GP7s and 270 GP9s, including B units. Don Wood photo

◂ Fog hangs over Altoona, Pennsylvania, as Pennsylvania Railroad TT-1, a westbound trailer train, changes crews at Works Tower on January 29, 1957. An inductive train phone antenna adorns the top of GP9 7000's long hood. Philip R. Hastings photo

◀◀ The Pennsy sprang for 40 cabless GP9Bs, all equipped with dynamic brakes. With a porthole instead of a cab, GP9B 7234B stands out from a mix of conventional Geeps lettered for N&W and Pennsy. David P. Morgan Library Collection

◀ Two of **Reading's** 44 GP7s push on a coal drag rolling through the Bethlehem, Pennsylvania, passenger station on April 10, 1966. Reading owned GP7s but no GP9s or GP18s. Victor Hand photo

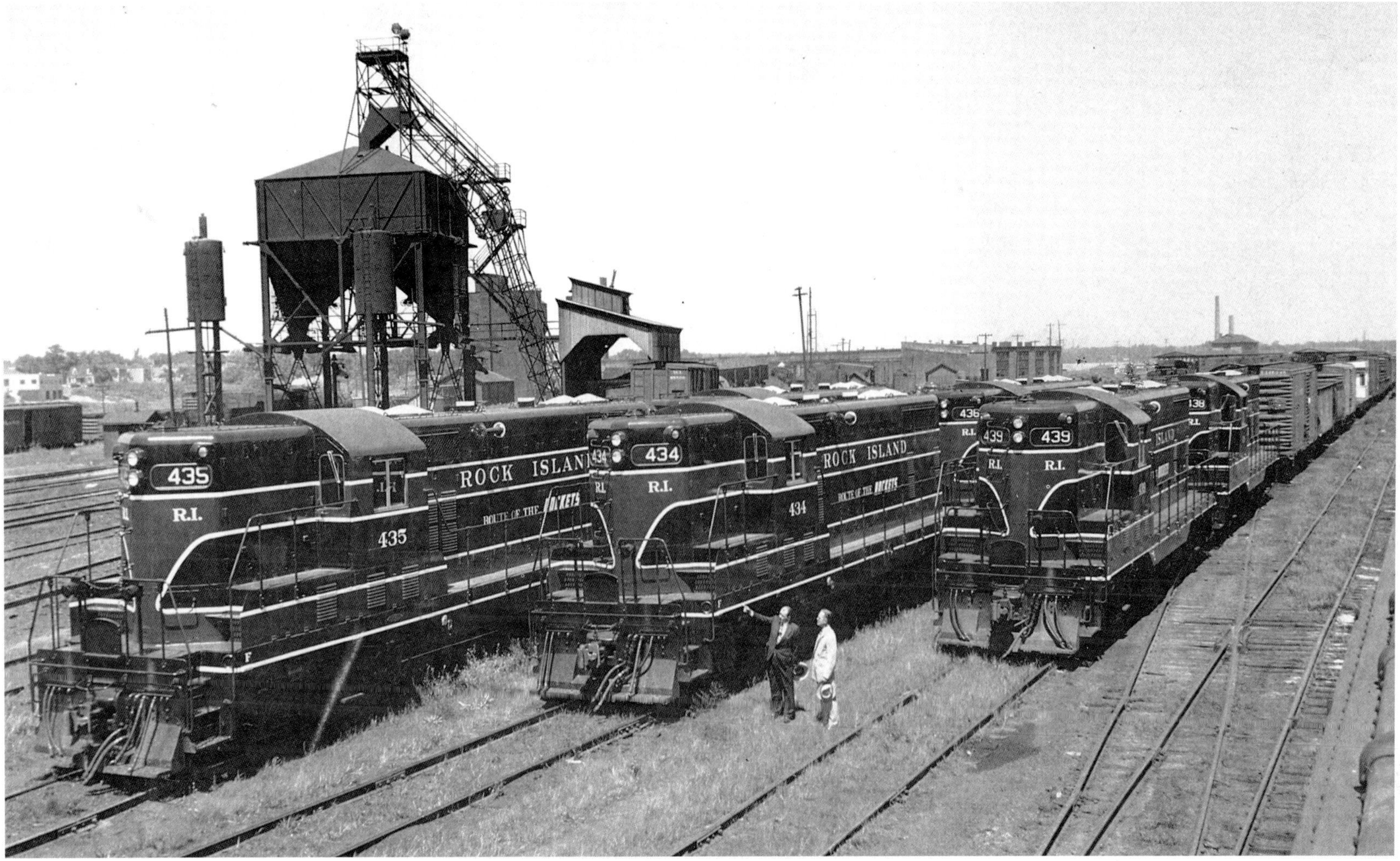

◀ Almost brand-new, back-to-back red, black, and white **Chicago, Rock Island & Pacific** GP7s storm through the Iowa hamlet of Stockton on September 14, 1952. The "Rock" took 112 GP7s built between 1950 and 1952. Charles H. Kerrigan photo

▲ Rock Island's Chicago-area terminal at Blue Island, Illinois, hosts a lineup of new GP7s on August 21, 1950. The Rock went back to EMD for 21 GP9s and 22 high-nosed GP18s (three rebuilt from wrecked GP7s and rated at 1,500 horsepower). Rock Island photo

▶ St. Louis-Southwestern's only GP7 304 sits with a local freight at Camden, Arkansas, on June 16, 1962. A subsidiary of Southern Pacific, SSW (known as the "Cotton Belt") contributed the only GP7 to SP's locomotive fleet. Steve Patterson photo

▶▶ Four olive drab and yellow Geeps lead **Seaboard Air Line** freight No. 88, (dubbed "the Ironmaster") through Rockmart, Georgia, in May 1953. SAL owned 123 GP7s built between May 1950 and September 1952. R. D. Sharpless photo

▶ Seaboard Air Line train 280 eases past Main Street Station in Richmond, Virginia, in October 1961. Unit 1927 shows the twin 48-inch cooling fans typical of late GP9 production. J. Parker Lamb photo

▶▶ An Alco RSC-3 (a six-axle, four-motor road-switcher rated at 1,600 horsepower) punctuates a pair of Seaboard Air Line Geeps on train No. 78, shown leaving the yard at Hamlet, North Carolina, in May 1962. SAL took title to 56 GP9s and 10 GP18s. J. Parker Lamb photo

 ▲ Under the gaze of Great Lakes boat *Ernest T. Weir*, a maroon and gold GP9 belonging to the **Minneapolis, St. Paul & Sault Ste. Marie** heads up train No. 7 at Sault Ste. Marie, Michigan, in September 1955. Jim Scribbins photo

▲ Soo Line GP9s 409 and 408 stand ready to lead westbound Soo time freight No. 25 (known as the "Western Soo-per") out of Shoreham Yard in Minneapolis, Minnesota, on May 11, 1958. Soo sampled 7 GP7s as appetizers, then chowed down on 45 GP9s. William D. Middleton photo

▶ **Southern Pacific** liked GP9s enough to buy 340 units, all equipped with dynamic brakes. SP's total includes 73 for subsidiary Texas & New Orleans and 12 more for the Cotton Belt. Robert Hale photo

▶▶ Southern Pacific GP9 5604 emerged from EMD in January 1955. Three different lights on the end of the Geep's short hood offer additional visibility at grade crossings, a typical SP diesel option. Robert Hale photo

▶ SP subsidiaries come face to face in Addison, Texas, as Texas & New Orleans GP9 438 meets Cotton Belt 825 on June 18, 1963. All SP system Geeps wore the "black widow" scheme trimmed in orange and silver. Steve Patterson photo

▶▶ Four GP9s pump up the train air on Southern Pacific TOFC (trailer on flat car) train 374 at San Jose, California, in 1958. The train, destined for Los Angeles, includes cars from No. 336, which arrived earlier from SP's East Bay terminal at Oakland. Richard Steinheimer photo

▶ Headed south with 114 loads, green and white **Southern Railway** GP7 2179 leads train 153 (Potomac Yard–New Orleans) through a cut near Enterprise, Mississippi, on June 24, 1955. J. Parker Lamb photo

▶▶ An eastbound Southern Railway freight glides over a bridge near Corona, Alabama, behind two GP7s in November 1960. Like Santa Fe, Southern grasped the road-switcher concept early and bought more GP7s than GP9s. The lead unit is in the newer black and white scheme. William S. Young photo

▶ A freight pulled by blue and gray EMD F units rolls into **Texas & Pacific**'s yard in Fort Worth, Texas, as black and gold GP7 1113 looks on. T&P bought 21 GP7s, 14 GP9s, and 5 low-nose GP18s. Linn H. Westcott photo

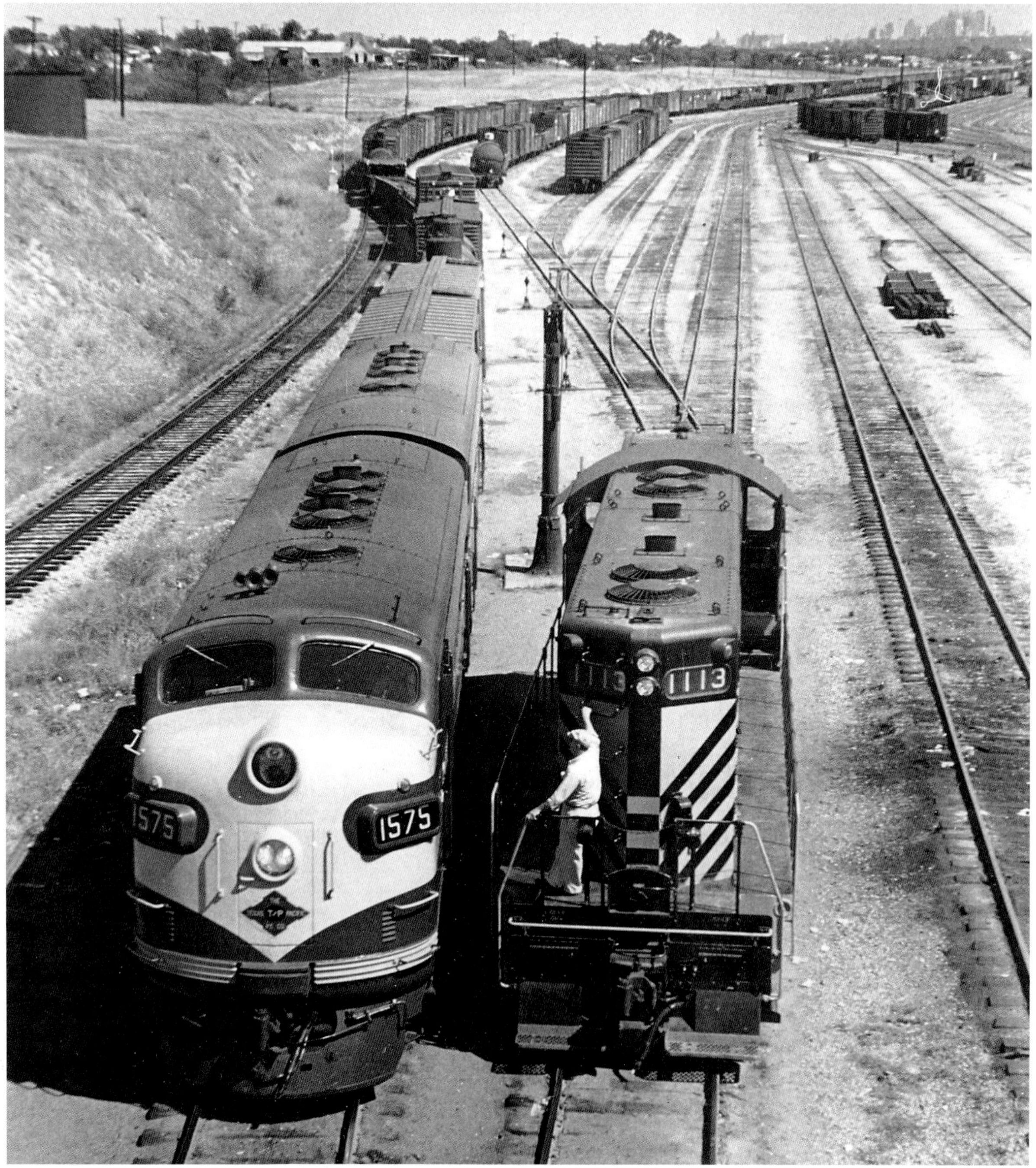

◀ **Toledo, Peoria & Western's** entire fleet of GP7s, painted olive drab and gold, moves a westbound local freight through Kolbe, Illinois, west of Peoria, on October 3, 1960. The "Tip-up" skipped GP9s and settled on a single low-nose GP18 for its next Geep purchase. J. Parker Lamb photo

▲ **Union Pacific** GP9 134 and GP9B 131B arrive in North Platte, Nebraska, on February 12, 1954, one of 75 such sets ordered by UP. All UP units were Armour yellow and gray with red trim. Photo by Art Stensvad

▶ Union Pacific 173 is one of an order for 75 UP GP9s built between February and April 1954. Unlike Santa Fe and Southern, UP owned more GP9s (344 units, including cabless versions) than GP7s (30 units). Union Pacific Railroad photo

▶ Union Pacific train 19 rolls through the upper Columbia River gorge near Wallula, Washington, in June 1965. Steam-generator-equipped GP7 128 sports a revised long hood with lowered number boards, a snowplow, and boxy exhaust stack spark arresters. Richard Steinheimer photo

▶▶ Eleven years and four months after it was built, UP GP9 255 rolls northbound train BFU through Cache Junction, Utah, in March 1966. The freight is bound for Pocatello. Richard Steinheimer photo

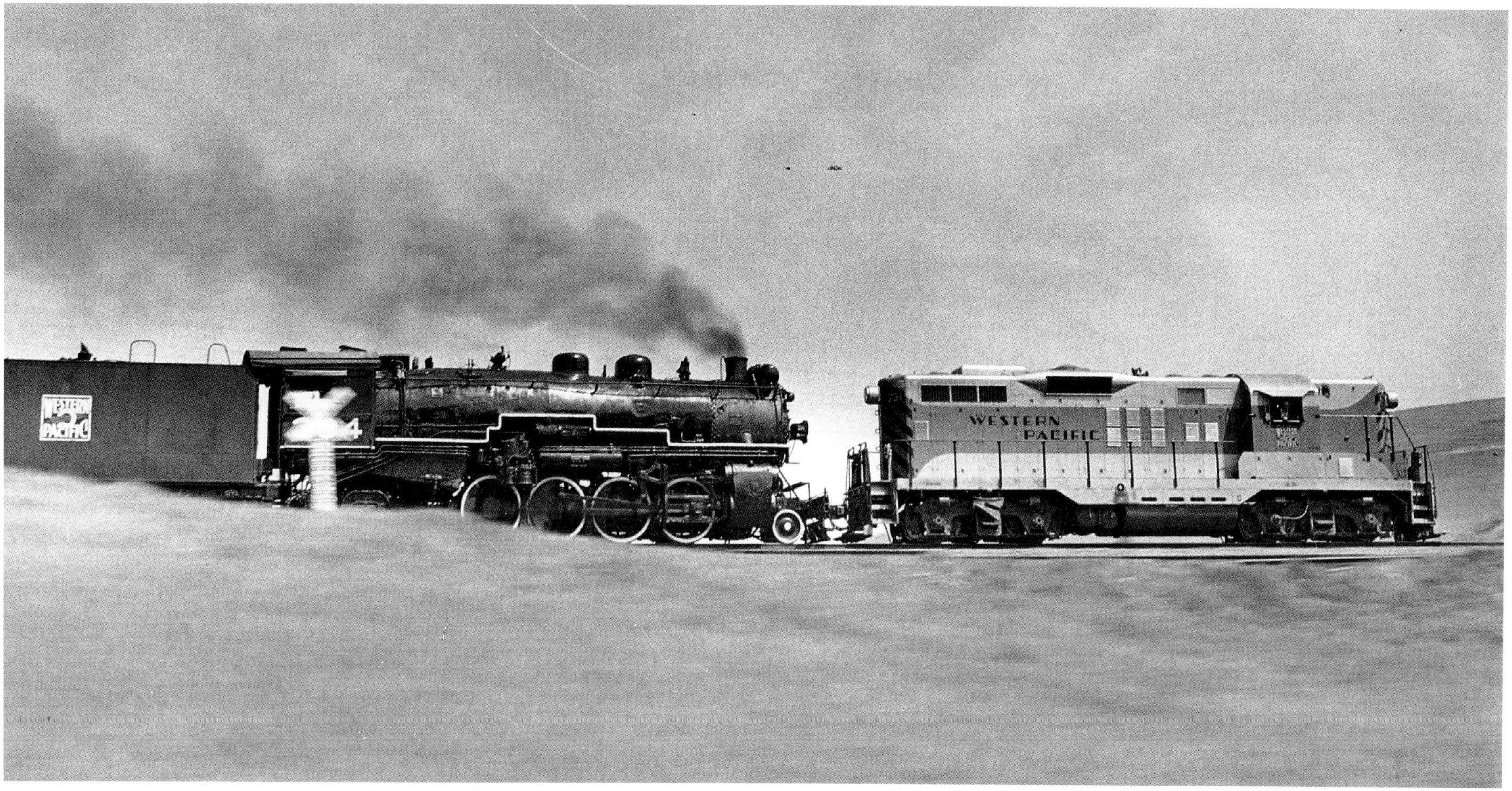

◄ With one car and a caboose in tow, **Wabash** GP7 470, painted gray, dark blue, and white, rolls through a fallow cornfield near Danville, Illinois, on April 7, 1958. Wabash bought 34 GP7s and 12 GP9s. J. Parker Lamb photo

▲ **Western Pacific** favored EMD cab units for freight and passenger service and bought only eight GP9s, all equipped with dynamic brakes, all built in September 1955. Robert Hale photo

▶ The interlocking tower at the SP-WP crossing in Niles, California, guards the passage of a westbound freight behind WP 725, the railroad's first Geep. The Geep's headlight is not that from a WP steam engine, but simply a large cylindrical headlight thought to be better suited to mountain railroading. WP's units were painted orange and silver with black striping. J. W. Swanberg photo

Geeps Today

◂ Chicago & North Western GP7 4190 heads west through Chicago's Western Avenue interlocking plant with a lone boxcar. One of more than 100 former Rock Island units purchased by C&NW after the Rock's demise in 1980, it was one of three Geeps assigned to shuttle Metra commuter cars between the California Avenue coach yards and North Western Station in downtown Chicago. Andrew McBride photo

As I write these words in the spring of 2000, Union Pacific operates three Geeps, all former Chicago & North Western units, all assigned to California Avenue shops in Chicago for switching commuter trains.

Because they're limited to a specific assignment, UP's Geeps seldom, if ever, leave Chicago. Still, if someone called me today and said, "Hey, those three UP Geeps are taking a road freight to Milwaukee!" I'd be off the phone and trackside as fast as my legs could take me. That's because Geeps in revenue main line freight service are a rare sight at the dawn of the 21st century.

It wasn't always that way, of course. Geeps dominated the North American railroad scene during railroading's so-called "Golden Years" from the late 1940s to the early 1960s. Nonetheless, many railfan photographers shunned Geeps, leaving a hole in the photographic history of North American railroading, not to mention the David P. Morgan Memorial library (where most of the photos in this book came from). When I noted the absence of Geep photos, former Kalmbach librarian George Drury told me, "The steam guys didn't like diesels, and the rest only wanted to shoot cab units. Geeps were mundane." The result: If you don't find photos of your favorite railroad's Geeps in this book, it's likely because they weren't available for me to choose.

Fortunately, not every railfan photographer threw in the towel in the postwar years. This book contains a disproportionate number of photos by J. Parker Lamb, and for good reason: Parker didn't hesitate to shoot Geeps in the 1950s and early 1960s. Along with such dedicated "Golden Years" shooters as Herbert H. Harwood Jr., John C. Illman, Richard Steinheimer, and even Kalmbach founder A. C. Kalmbach, Lamb understood what songwriter Carly Simon meant when she sang, "These are the good old days." For everyone who cares about the history and documentation of railroading, we're the luckier for their efforts.

Acknowledgments

Thanks to Jane Brunette for her support and patience during the writing of this book; George H. Drury for proofreading and compiling the index; Michael R. Stephens for helping get the project off the ground (read: Getting me to commit to the project in the first place!); James Slocum for clearing a spot for me to work while pulling photos in Kalmbach's David P. Morgan Memorial Library; Andrew McBride for pitching in and helping me pull and organize photos; Dick Christianson for tolerating the "outlander" who invaded the Books Department for several weeks in March 2000 while I pulled photos; and my ever-patient, always helpful editor, Kent Johnson (who allowed me to slip in a plug for American Flyer's S gauge GP7 despite his allegiance to O gauge!).

Paul Schneider
Milwaukee, Wisconsin

Index of Photographs

Railroads
Aberdeen & Rockfish, 21
Alaska Railroad, 13
Atchison, Topeka & Santa Fe, 22–24
Atlantic Coast Line, 20
Baltimore & Ohio, 26, 27
Bangor & Aroostook, 25
Belt Railway of Chicago, 28
Boston & Maine, 17, 29, 30
Canadian National, 15, 37
Canadian Pacific, 40
Central of Georgia, 32
Central Railroad of New Jersey, 39
Central Vermont, 38
Chesapeake & Ohio, 44, 45
Chicago & Eastern Illinois, 33
Chicago & North Western, 9, 15, 42, 43, 125
Chicago, Burlington & Quincy, 31
Chicago, Milwaukee, St. Paul & Pacific, 9, 34–36
Chicago, Rock Island & Pacific, 4, 17, 100, 101
Cotton Belt, see St. Louis Southwestern
Delaware, Lackawanna & Western, 13, 51
Denver & Rio Grande Western, 46, 47
Detroit & Toledo Shore Line, 49

Detroit, Toledo & Ironton, 48
Erie Lackawanna, 51, 52
Erie, 50
Frisco, see St. Louis-San Francisco
Georgia Railroad, 55
Grand Trunk Western, 15, 56
Great Northern, 13, 57–59
Illinois Central, 11, 60–63
Illinois Terminal, 64, 65
Lehigh Valley, 69, 70, 84, 85
Louisville & Nashville, 9, 13, 66–68
Maine Central, 71
Milwaukee Road, see Chicago, Milwaukee, St. Paul & Pacific
Minneapolis & St. Louis, 76
Minneapolis, St. Paul & Sault Ste. Marie, 9, 106, 107
Missouri Pacific, 17, 73–75
Missouri-Kansas-Texas, 72
Nashville, Chattanooga & St. Louis, 77
New York Central, 25, 79–83
New York, Chicago & St. Louis, 84–87
New York, New Haven & Hartford, 15
New York, Susquehanna & Western, 94–95
Nickel Plate Road, see New York, Chicago & St. Louis
Norfolk & Western, 88–91
Northern Pacific, 15, 92, 93

Pennsylvania Railroad, 97, 98
Peoria & Eastern, 80, 81, 83
Phelps-Dodge Corp., 78
Quanah, Acme & Pacific, 53
Reading, 99
Rock Island, see Chicago, Rock Island & Pacific
Santa Fe, see Atchison, Topeka & Santa Fe
Seaboard Air Line, 103–105
Soo Line, see Minneapolis, St. Paul & Sault Ste. Marie
Southern Pacific, 9, 15, 108–111
Southern Railway, 9, 112, 113
St. Louis Southwestern, 102, 110
St. Louis-San Francisco, 53, 54
Texas & New Orleans, 110
Texas & Pacific, 114
Toledo, Peoria & Western, 115
Union Pacific, 9, 116, 117, 118, 119
Wabash, 120
Western Pacific, 121, 122

Locomotive types
BL2, 4, 5
B (cabless) units, 15, 23, 98, 116
GP7 (by road number)
    ACL 261, 20
    AT&SF 2691, 22

AT&SF 2791, 23
AT&SF 2812, 24
BAR 69/70, 15
BRC 470, 28
C&EI 211/227/229, 33
C&NW 1565, 42
C&NW 1520, 43
C&NW 4190, 125
C&O 5747, 44
CB&Q 213/262, 31
CN 4366, 37
CN 4370, 38
CNJ 1526, 39
CRI&P 434/435/436/438/439, 101
CRI&P 1257/1259, 100
D&TSL 46, 49
DL&W 952, 13
DT&I 957, 48
EL 1400, 51
EL 1403, 52
EMD 100, 3, 8, 9, 10
EMD 200, 9
EMD 300, 9, 11
EMD 922, 8
ERIE 1241, 50
GN 639, 13
GN 642/644, 57
IC 8800, 60
ITC 1602/1605, 65

ITC 1604/1605, 64
L&N 422/433, 66
L&N 505, 13
L&N 550, 67
MKT 1512, 72
MP 4149, 73
MP 4305, 74
MP 4321, 75
NC&StL 719, 720, 77
NP 557, 92
NYC 5613, 81
NYC 5621/5622, 80
NYC 5625, 83
NYC 5827, 82
P&E 5613, 81
P&E 5621/5622, 80
P&E 5625, 83
RDG 612/622, 99
SAL 1814, 103
SLSF 507, 53
SLSF 522, 54
SLSW 304, 102
SR 2179, 112
SR 6544, 113
T&P 1113, 114
TP&W 102/103, 115
U. S. Army 1826, 15
UP 128, 118
WAB 470, 120

GP7B (by road number)
AT&SF 2791A, 23

GP9 (by road number)
BAR 76, 15
B&M 1708, 30
B&O 3414, 27
B&O 6452/6459, 26
C&NW 1714, 15
C&O 6091/6155/6188, 45
CMStP&P 204/208, 35
CofG 166, 32
CP 8662, 40
D&RGW 5912, 47
D&RGW 5912/5913/5914, 46
GA 1026/1040, 3130
GN 690/721/729, 59
GTW 1754, 15, 56
IC 9109, 62
IC 9049, 63
IC 9059/9094, 61
LV 301, 70
M&StL 706, 76
MStP&SSteM 408/409, 107
MStP&SSteM 552, 106
N&W 711, 88, 90–91
N&W 710/712/713, 90–91
N&W 2708, 89
NP 318, 93
NP 376, 15
NYC 5963, 79
NYC 5979, 81
NYC&StL 454/472, 86
NYC&StL 520, 87
NYC&StL 529, 86
NYC&StL 812/814, 84, 85
NYNH&H, 15
Phelps-Dodge 21, 78
PRR 7000, 97
PRR 7012/7024, 96
SAL 1920, 105
SAL 1927, 104
SLSW 825, 110
SP 438, 110
SP 3726, 15
SP 5604, 109
T&NO 438, 110
UP 134, 116
UP 173, 117
UP 255, 119
WP 725, 122

GP9B (by road number)
PRR 7234B, 98
UP 131B, 116

UP 326B, 15

GP18 (by road number)
A&R 300, 21
B&M 1770, 17
B&M 1753, 29
EMD 1800, 17
L&N 460, 68
LV 303, 69
MP 433, 17
N&W 962, 98
NYS&W 1800/1802/1804, 94–95

RS-1, 6

Photographers
Alford, Hayden T., 66
Anderson, Clyde L, 54
Atchison, Topeka & Santa Fe, 23
Brennan, William J., 69
Chesapeake & Ohio, 45
Chicago & North Western, 43
Chicago, Rock Island & Pacific, 101
Clarkson, Bob, 89
Dutch, Thomas O., 73
Ehlbeck, Henry J., 50
Electro-Motive Division, 13, 15, 17, 56
Francis, Philip D., 52
Fredrickson, Jim, 93
Gray, Johnnie, M., 74
Gruber, John, 28
Hale, Robert, 46, 108, 109, 121
Hand, Victor, 55, 99
Harwood, Herbert H., Jr., 26, 79, 82, 87
Hastings, Philip R., 49, 97
Hofsommer, Don, 76
Illman, John C., 31, 37
Ingles, J. David, 15, 48
Kalmbach, A. C., 77
Kanak, Edward, 58
Kerrigan, Charles H., 100
Kistler, Stan, 22
Lamb, J. Parker, intro, 20, 21, 27, 32, 33, 60, 67, 86, 104, 105, 112, 115, 120
Lloyd, G. E., 80
Louisville & Nashville, 68
Love, Betty, 75
Marre, Louis A., 5
McBride, Andrew, 125
Meyer, Bruce R., 81, 88
Middleton, William D., 61, 62, 63, 64, 93, 107
Patterson, Steve, 102, 110
Peters, Walter A., 65
Plowden, David, 38, 39
Plummer, R. S., 72
Priebe, Norman, 13, 57
Rogoza, Carl, 70
Schafer, Mike, 40
Scott, Fred, 83
Scribbins, Jim, 106
Sharpless, R. D., 103
Shaughnessy, Jim, 29, 30, 71
Sims, Donald, 53, 78
Steinheimer, Richard, 24, 36, 47, 59, 111, 118, 119
Stensvad, Art, 116
Swanberg, J. W., 122–123
Trager, George A., 15
Union Pacific, 117
Westcott, Linn H., 114
Witbeck, C. W., 11
Wood, Don, 96
Young, J. J., Jr., 84, 85
Young, William S., 51, 94–95, 113